CHOCOLA
MEMORABILIA

DONNA S. BAKER

4880 Lower Valley Road, Atglen, PA 19310 USA

Dedication

Fine friends, like fine chocolate, enrich one's life immeasurably. This book is for Isabel, who is not only my very dear friend, but a most unabashed chocoholic!

Designed by "Sue"
Type set in BernhardMod BT/Korinna BT

ISBN: 0-7643-1153-0
Printed in China
1 2 3 4

"Wilbur Buds" and "Buds" are registered trademarks of the Wilbur Chocolate Co., Inc., Lititz, Pa.

Published by Schiffer Publishing Ltd.
4880 Lower Valley Road
Atglen, PA 19310
Phone: (610) 593-1777; Fax: (610) 593-2002
E-mail: Schifferbk@aol.com
Please visit our web site catalog at
www.schifferbooks.com
We are always looking for people to write books on new and related subjects. If you have an idea for a book, please contact us at the above address.

This book may be purchased from the publisher.
Include $3.95 for shipping.
Please try your bookstore first.
You may write for a free catalog.

In Europe, Schiffer books are distributed by
Bushwood Books
6 Marksbury Ave.
Kew Gardens
Surrey TW9 4JF England
Phone: 44 (0) 20 8392-8585
Fax: 44 (0) 20 8392-9876
E-mail: Bushwd@aol.com
Free postage in the UK. Europe: air mail at cost.

Contents

Acknowledgments

This book would not have been possible without the generous and much appreciated cooperation of the Wilbur Chocolate Candy Americana Museum and Store, a chocolate lover's haven located on the site of the Wilbur Chocolate Company in Lititz, Pennsylvania. I am especially indebted to store manager Michelle Havrilla, who lent her enthusiasm and vivacity to the project from the beginning, gave up a host of Sundays to help with photographing the wonderful contents of the museum, and supplied me with (real) chocolate inspiration throughout the process. Thank you, Michelle!

I am also most grateful to the staff of the Candy Americana Museum and Store for always making me feel welcome; to Margaret Madigan, Nancy Schiffer, and Brandi Wright for their help with recording information about the objects photographed; and to Lorry Hanes of Dad's Follies for graciously assisting with the chocolate mold section. And a special thank you is in order to

Penny Buzzard, whose dedication and love of chocolate and candy memorabilia led her to found the Candy Americana Museum back in 1972, so that others could appreciate these wonderfully engaging objects as well.

A visit to Wilbur's museum and store is a delightful (and delicious) experience, one you should not miss if you are traveling to the area. A mail order service and Internet site are also available:

Wilbur Chocolate Candy Americana Museum, Store, and
    Mail Order
48 North Broad Street
Lititz, Pennsylvania 17543
Toll free: 1-888-2WILBUR (294-5287)
(717) 626-3249 (store)
(717) 626-3226 (mail order)

Or "visit" on the Internet: www.wilburbuds.com

Introduction

Chocolate. The very word rolls off the tongue with a smoothness and luxuriousness befitting the extraordinary flavor it describes. The subject of countless cookbooks, the downfall of otherwise determined dieters, chocolate has enjoyed an undisputed and unrivaled reputation for centuries as the favorite of those born with a proverbial sweet tooth. A world without chocolate would be a bleak world indeed!

The origins of this incredibly popular substance are as exotic as the taste itself. The early Mayans, who flourished in what is now Mexico and Central America from about the third to the ninth centuries A.D., are credited with being the first to discover that the humble looking beans produced by the cacoa tree could be transformed into a most agreeable drink. The Mayans, and later the Aztecs, enjoyed chocolate as a spicy beverage, however, unlike the sweetened version we are accustomed to today. So prized were the cacao (or cocoa) beans used for making chocolate that the Mayans also used them as a form of currency. This, in fact, remained the primary use of cocoa beans as their popularity spread north from the Mayans to the Aztecs, an empire renowned as much for its ornate temples and palaces as for Montezuma II, the powerful leader who ruled from 1502 to 1520.

Montezuma and the elite of his empire continued to partake of the wondrous *xocoatl,* the name they gave to the drink prepared by mixing ground cocoa beans and water (and from which the contemporary term "chocolate" is derived). Legend has it that Montezuma drank his *xocoatl*—spiced with vanilla, honey, or sometimes chili powder—out of golden goblets, sometimes downing fifty at a time before retiring to his harem. Is it any wonder that Hernando Cortez, the Spanish conquistador who first visited Montezuma's court in 1519, was both intrigued and impressed with this heretofore unknown elixir?

Unlike Christopher Columbus (who reportedly brought back a few cocoa beans to Spain in 1502 but did not recognize their significance), Cortez carefully studied the Aztec's use of chocolate and returned to Spain in 1528 eager to share his enjoyment of this New World delicacy with the court of King Charles V. Once introduced to chocolate, the King and his countrymen were as enthusiastic as Cortez and chocolate soon became a favored drink of the Spaniards—though they modified the Aztec's recipe by using hot water instead of cold.

So enamored of chocolate were the Spaniards, that they chose not to share their newfound pleasure with the rest of Europe. The cocoa beans were imported from countries then under Spain's rule and processed by monks in secluded Spanish monasteries—who presumably could be trusted to maintain a shroud of secrecy over their work. Though it is hard to imagine in today's fast paced world, almost a hundred years went by before other countries began to get a whiff of Spain's clandestine chocolate manufacture. In the early 1600s, however, the "secret" began to leak out. Italy was the first of Spain's European neighbors to become acquainted with chocolate, perhaps from an enterprising traveler who brought back samples to share with his Italian friends. Now the popularity of chocolate spread quickly: though it remained primarily a drink enjoyed by the upper classes, chocolate was soon being sipped with pleasure (and often in fashionable clubs established just for that purpose) by the Austrians, French, Germans, and English. And though some still preferred chocolate with a tangy taste (one Prussian king is reported to have mixed pepper and mustard with his), much of the chocolate consumed by Europeans in the seventeenth century was sweetened with sugar and mixed with milk, rather than water.

Not until the eighteenth century did chocolate's allure make its way back across the Atlantic Ocean to colonial North America. While it may have been imported as early as 1712, chocolate was not well known in the colonies until after 1750 or so. As in Europe, however, it did not take long for the popularity of this novel beverage to grow (chocolate in beverage form was still the primary way to enjoy its taste; "eating chocolate" would not be available until many years later). Chocolate historians Sophie and Michael Coe note that "By the mid-18th century, Massachusetts sea captains were bringing back cacao beans from the tropics as cargo, for there was already a chocolate-drinking public in New England." (Coe, 1996, 230) To accommodate that eager public, two forward thinking entrepreneurs from Dorchester, Massachusetts, Dr. James Baker and John Hannon, established America's first chocolate factory in 1765. Although they originally marketed their product as Hannon's Best Chocolate, the company was later renamed the Walter Baker Company after being taken over in 1820 by James Baker's grandson, Walter. The success of Baker's company no doubt paved the way for many of the chocolate manufacturers who followed—many still very much in operation today.

Eight years after Walter Baker assumed leadership of his grandfather's chocolate factory, a momentous event in chocolate history took place in faraway Amsterdam. There, in 1828, a chemist named C.J. Van Houten patented his new invention: the cocoa press. Up to this point, there had been no practical means of extracting cocoa butter, a naturally occurring fat, from the ground up cocoa beans. With Van Houten's cocoa press, however, manufacturers could now separate out a high percentage of the cocoa butter, leaving behind a solid "cake" of chocolate that was then pulverized into a high quality cocoa. The impact of the cocoa press on the chocolate industry was revolutionary. It improved the solubility of chocolate in milk, giving the resulting drink a more pleasing consistency; it lowered the cost of manufacture, presaging the era of "chocolate for the masses;" and, perhaps most significantly, it gave chocolate manufacturers a means of creating chocolate in solid form by using the leftover cocoa butter—chocolate candy was about to become a reality!

Wooden box for Baker's Breakfast Cocoa, made by Walter Baker & Co. This Massachusetts company was originally known as Hannon's Best Chocolate and was the first chocolate factory established in America.

The British company of J.S. Fry & Sons, first established in the mid-1700s, is generally credited with being the first manufacturer to successfully create what we now know (and love!) as the chocolate candy bar. Already a leader in the industry, J.S. Fry & Sons capitalized on the new techniques made possible by the cocoa press to advance the chocolate world to an even grander level. Though experimentation had been going on for a while,

> [a] milestone was passed in 1847, when the Fry firm found a way to mix a blend of cocoa powder and sugar with melted cacao butter . . . instead of with warm water; this produced a thinner, less viscous paste which could be cast into a mold. The resulting chocolate bars, which they christened 'Chocolat Délicieux à Manger' (French-sounding food had a considerable cachet by this time), were exhibited in Birmingham in 1849. Apart from the pastilles [flavored tablets] and bars of 18th-century France, which were brittle and dry, and impossible to mold, this was the world's first true *eating* chocolate. (Coe, 1996, 243)

Another milestone in chocolate history took place some thirty years later, when a Swiss chocolate maker named Daniel Peter introduced the world to milk chocolate, a variation that continues to be immensely popular. Peter's innovative product was the result of his collaboration with Henri Nestlé, a Swiss chemist who had developed a process for making evaporated milk in 1867. Nestlé, of course, is a name well known throughout the world today, as the Nestlé Company went on to become one of the most prolific manufacturers of both chocolate and other food products worldwide.

By the late nineteenth and early twentieth centuries, the steps involved in chocolate manufacture for the mass market were well developed and the confectionery industry in both Europe and America was flourishing. Many of today's premier chocolatiers first opened their doors at this time; others already in business expanded their operations or their variety of products. Familiar names from Europe include Cadbury's of Great Britain, Droste of Holland, Tobler, Lindt, and the aforementioned Nestlé

of Switzerland—all in business since the middle or end of the nineteenth century. In America, Milton Hershey had already established a successful caramel business in Pennsylvania when he attended the 1893 World's Columbian Exposition in Chicago. There he was captivated by a display of European chocolate machinery—within ten years he had sold his caramel business and was well on his way to becoming one of the world's most memorable names in chocolate. E.J. Brach & Sons, Whitman's Chocolate, and Ghirardelli are other well known American companies whose forays into chocolate began around the same time or even earlier.

Tucked away in the picturesque Pennsylvania Dutch town of Lititz, the Wilbur Chocolate Company also traces its history to the late nineteenth century and is a wonderful example of how a small, family run chocolate business developed over the years into one of today's leading manufacturers of chocolate products for confectioners, dairies, and candy makers all across America. A glimpse at some of Wilbur's colorful advertising, packaging, and manufacturing memorabilia—all presented in the chapters to follow—affords chocolate aficionados a delightful view not only of Wilbur's fascinating past but also that of its sister chocolate companies. For while each company is certainly unique, each shares a common link to the societal trends and tastes of the times. And each, like this book, celebrates the joys of chocolate every day!

About the Values

The values listed in this book are intended to provide readers with a general idea of what they might expect to pay for the same or similar item in today's market. The values represent a guideline only and are not meant to "set" prices in any way. It is entirely possible to purchase an item for a higher or lower amount than the value shown here, as many factors affect the actual price paid. These factors include condition, scarcity, the location of the market, and the buyer's relative desire to own a particular item. Items not priced in this book are contemporary or modern and therefore do not yet have a secondary market value.

The "Centennial Building" of Croft, Wilbur & Co. was
located at 1226 Market Street in Philadelphia.

Chapter One
The Wilbur Chocolate Company—A Brief History

One of Lititz, Pennsylvania's most charming attractions, the present day Wilbur Chocolate Company dates back to the late nineteenth century and—like many of its contemporaries—has gone through a variety of name and location changes through the years. The company's founder was an enterprising businessman named Henry Oscar (H.O.) Wilbur, who originally pursued his livelihood in the stove and hardware business. Though this business was apparently quite successful, Wilbur was drawn to new ventures in the confectionery trade and found a willing partner in candy manufacturer Samuel Croft. In 1865 the two men entered into partnership and opened a Philadelphia candy business known as Croft, Wilbur & Co., producing mostly molasses candies and hard candies over a period of nearly twenty years. The business prospered, leading the partners to move from their origi-

nal location on North Third Street to larger facilities at 1226 Market Street. Although Croft, Wilbur & Co. did include some chocolate among their products, they are perhaps best known for producing what is thought to be the very first glass candy container, a replica of the Liberty Bell that was filled with candy and sold at the 1876 Centennial Exposition held in Philadelphia.

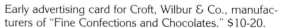

Early advertising card for Croft, Wilbur & Co., manufacturers of "Fine Confections and Chocolates." $10-20.

Three 5 lb. tins of Celebrated Cough Drops, manufactured by Croft, Wilbur & Co., Philadelphia, Pa. 6.75" high, $35-50 ea.

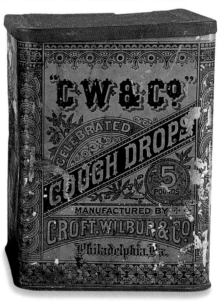

H.O. Wilbur must have known that his destiny lay in the world of chocolate, however, for in 1884 he and Samuel Croft decided to split their business in two: Croft would continue manufacturing candy with a new partner under the name of Croft & Allen, while Wilbur—now operating as H.O. Wilbur & Sons—would concentrate on the manufacture of cocoa and chocolate products. As one would expect from the new company's name, H.O. Wilbur was assisted in this new chocolate business by his three sons: William, Harry, and Bertram (although Bertram, a physician, did not become actively involved in the company until the death of Harry in 1900).

In 1887, H.O. Wilbur & Sons needed more room for their flourishing business and the company moved to yet another location in Philadelphia, this one at Third, New and Bread Streets. That same year, the company's charming logo known as the "stirring cupid" first made its appearance—this little winged cupid with his bow and arrows stirring a steaming cup of cocoa subsequently became one of Wilbur's most enduring and well known images. Another fortuitous event occurred just six years later, when the company introduced what is still their most famous product for the retail market—the delightful Wilbur Buds. Here's how the origin of this product (and its name!) is described on the back of a contemporary Wilbur Buds box:

It was 1894 when Mr. H.O. Wilbur, looking for ways to sell more chocolate from his locally famous confectionery business in Philadelphia, hit upon a unique concept. He developed a process whereby he could "deposit" his specially blended and "aged" chocolate into a unique solid shape that very much resembled a flower bud.

People immediately began gobbling up Mr. Wilbur's delectable bite size "Wilbur Buds" at such a rate that soon his factory had to be expanded to handle the demand! All through the 1800's and early 1900's Wilbur Buds enjoyed local fame. Mr. Wilbur truly personified the American spirit of quality and innovation.

DELAWARE RIVER BRIDGE BETWEEN PHILADELPHIA, PA. AND CAMDEN. N. J.

61748

One of H.O. Wilbur's several Philadelphia locations is illustrated on this postcard of the Delaware River Bridge and its surrounding buildings. $10-20.

Black and white photograph showing an early—and certainly eye-catching—means of promoting Wilbur's Chocolate Buds! Photograph, $40-50.

10

Around the same time that Wilbur Buds were first being enjoyed by Philadelphia chocolate lovers, another chocolate manufacturer was setting up business just a few hours to the west. The Kendig Chocolate Company, originally founded as a caramel factory, opened for business in c. 1900 in the small Pennsylvania town of Lititz, about eight miles from Lancaster. The company operated under the name of Kendig for a short time only, however; in 1902 it was sold to new owners and became known as the Ideal Cocoa and Chocolate Company. Not long afterwards a new plant was constructed at 48 North Broad Street in Lititz, just adjacent to the Reading and Columbia railroad station. Interestingly, and perhaps prophetically, the name change to Ideal Cocoa and Chocolate is reported to have occurred on February 14, 1902—the date on which Valentine's Day is historically celebrated. Today, of course, gifts of fine chocolate are highly coveted on this most romantic of holidays!

Early postcards showing the Ideal Cocoa and Chocolate Company at 48 North Broad Street in Lititz, Pennsylvania. "I can't believe the architects planned it that way," wrote a descendant of one of Ideal's employees, "but due to the window screens in the three top floors of the building and prevailing west winds, all areas east of the building have been blessed through the years with the delicious aromas of chocolate manufacturing." (Muth, 1982, 3) $40-60 ea.

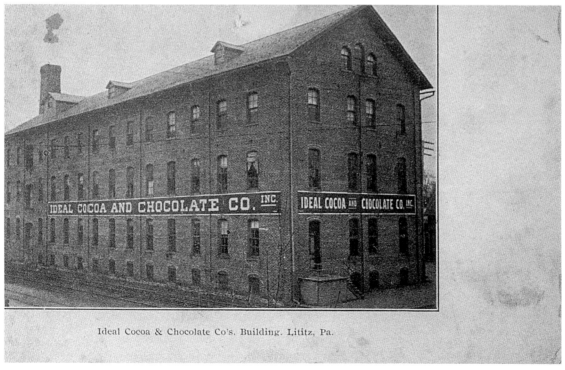

Ideal Cocoa & Chocolate Co's. Building. Lititz, Pa.

11

Whether February 14 was selected by coincidence or design is not known, of course, but the Ideal Cocoa and Chocolate Co. proved successful and became noted for such products as Chocolate Cigars, Nut Lunch bars, Ideal Almond Bars, Noah's Arks, and Ideal Cocoa. Although one historian reports that Milton Hershey, founder of the nearby Hershey's Chocolate, was among Ideal's prospective buyers around 1913 (Muth, 1982, 2), the company remained in business until December 2, 1927, when it merged with the Brewster Chocolate Co. of Newark, New Jersey to become the Brewster-Ideal Chocolate Co.

Back in Philadelphia, changes were occurring for H.O. Wilbur & Sons as well, and its path was about to converge with that of Brewster-Ideal. In the late 1920s, H.O. Wilbur & Sons had begun negotiating with the Suchard Société Anonyme of Switzerland for the right to manufacture and sell world renowned Suchard chocolate. The rights to this process were finally obtained in 1928 and with it came a change in the company's name from H.O. Wilbur & Sons, Inc. to Wilbur-Suchard Chocolate Company, Inc. At the same time, the newly dubbed Wilbur-Suchard Chocolate Company merged with the Brewster-Ideal Chocolate Company, thus uniting the history of H.O. Wilbur & Sons with that of the Kendig Chocolate Company, the Ideal Cocoa and Chocolate Company, and the Brewster Chocolate Company.

From 1928 through 1934, the Wilbur-Suchard Chocolate Company operated out of three locations (Philadelphia, site of the original H.O. Wilbur factory; Newark, site of the original Brewster factory; and Lititz, site of the original Ideal factory); by 1934, however, all

Postcard showing the front of the building, after the 1928 name change to Wilbur-Suchard. $40-60.

A lone salesman tends this trade show display for Wilbur-Suchard Chocolate Co. / Brewster-Ideal Chocolate Co., c. late 1920s. Photograph, $40-50.

operations had been consolidated in Lititz. During their thirty years of business, Wilbur-Suchard produced a full line of chocolate products for both the retail and wholesale markets and were especially noted for their Suchard line of chocolate squares and bars. The company promoted their Suchard Chocolate Squares as "bite-size morsels of solid chocolate individually foil-wrapped and packed in beautifully colored, hermetically-sealed, moisture-proof, double cellophane bags to insure the utmost in freshness to the consumer." Chocolate fanciers could also purchase Suchard 5¢ Bars, 10¢ Bars, Suchard Villages (laminated foil "houses" filled with Milk Chocolate Squares), and, of course, the ever popular Wilbur Buds. Company literature from c. 1940 describes the Buds as "wonderful bits of goodness made under a formula more than fifty years' old to produce a rich dark vanilla chocolate of outstanding character." Wilbur Buds, the company warned, were known as a habit-forming chocolate— though it reassured consumers that this was a "pleasant and harmless habit" stemming from people's preference for Wilbur Buds over any other type of chocolate!

A large box of Wilbur Buds was prominently featured in this window display for Glassmyer's store. Photograph, $50-75.

Wilbur Chocolate employees posed for this group photo in 1927. Photograph, $20-30.

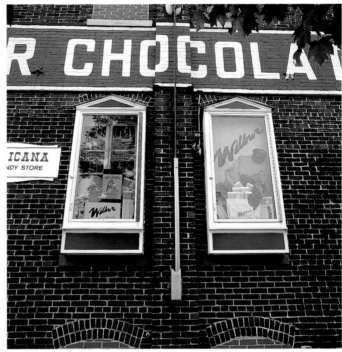

The Wilbur Chocolate Company today, still located at 48 North Broad Street in Lititz. Some of the items for sale at the outlet store are featured in the tall front windows.

Today, the company that began with H.O. Wilbur's propitious foray into the chocolate world is known as the Wilbur Chocolate Company and is still based in the red brick building at 48 North Broad Street in Lititz (a second manufacturing plant in the nearby town of Mt. Joy was acquired by Wilbur in 1982 from the Bachman Candy Co., which owned Peter Paul Cadbury). Wilbur's most recent name change became effective on January 1, 1959 and coincided with the company's celebration of its 75th Anniversary (1884-1959). In 1992, Wilbur was acquired as a wholly owned subsidiary by Cargill, Inc., a world-wide food processing corporation.

From the 1950s and 1960s to the present, Wilbur has been a leading manufacturer of chocolate coatings and other chocolate products used by candy manufacturers, bakeries, and dairies; in addition, the company still produces Wilbur Buds, Bars, Breakfast Cocoa and other treats for the chocolate-loving public. In the 1950s, Wilbur was a pioneer in both the intra- and inter-state delivery of liquid chocolate coatings through the use of "custom-built, controlled-heat tank trucks"; a 1959 trade journal article noted that this enabled the company to significantly enlarge its delivery area to a 700 mile radius around Lititz. Taste, as well as transportation, has also won kudos for Wilbur: early in its history the company won several World's Fair medals for its chocolate coatings, and in 1983 the *Chicago Tribune* reported that its sixteen member panel of chocolate experts ranked Wilbur's milk chocolate for baking as its top American choice in this category.

Behind Wilbur's red and green awning lies a special treat for visitors to the factory: the Candy Americana Museum started in 1972 by Penny Buzzard, wife of then

Wilbur president John Buzzard. Dedicated to the compilation of chocolate memorabilia of all types, the museum houses a wide assortment of early candy machinery, chocolate molds, candy boxes and tins, advertising, chocolate pots and more. Step inside with us now for a pictorial tour of this delightful tribute to America's ongoing love affair with chocolate . . .

Chapter Two
Manufacturing and Molds

Chocolate in its many forms originates with the cacao tree, a tropical plant that thrives in hot, humid climates and produces melon shaped pods filled with small, hard beans. The full botanical name of this rather delicate tree is *Theobroma Cacao*, meaning—aptly enough—"food of the gods."

Weighing about one pound each, the yellow or reddish brown pods grow on both the branches and trunks of the cacao tree. As the pods ripen, they swell—finally bursting to reveal the rather nondescript looking beans inside. In their initial state, these tiny seeds give little indication of their future potential. "Cocoa beans are not unlike pebbles in appearance," says one contemporary author. "If they fell out of a sack at your feet you probably would not give them a second glance . . . [yet] 'Brown gold' is the name that has been given to the product processed from the beans." (Teubner et. al., 1997, 22)

Cocoa pods, the melon shaped fruit of the cacao tree. One has been split to illustrate the formation of cocoa beans inside. A typical cocoa pod contains anywhere from twenty to fifty beans; approximately four hundred are required to make one pound of chocolate.

This old metal scoop is filled with unprocessed cocoa beans.

It was probably a serendipitous discovery on the part of early Indians that if the cacao pods fell to the damp earth and fermented there, the beans tasted far better than if left to dry out on the tree. Rather than wait for the pods to fall off on their own, the Indians no doubt began expediting the process by hacking them off with machetes, then tossing them on the ground to absorb the moisture and ferment. Despite today's modern manufacturing methods, harvesting of cacao pods from the trees is still done by hand, using machetes for pods growing on the trunk and long steel knives for those on the upper branches.

Tools used in the harvesting of cocoa beans. The wooden machete is from South America and was used to clear areas near the valuable cocoa trees. The long metal knife is from Africa and was used to cut cocoa pods from the trees.

While it is beyond the scope of this book to describe the chocolate manufacturing process in detail, it is interesting that the basic steps in the process—which include fermenting, drying, and roasting the beans, removing the outer shells, and grinding the remaining "nibs" to a smooth, liquid consistency—have remained largely intact since the turn of the twentieth century (though technological advancements have, of course, changed the "look" of each of these steps). Here is how the Wilbur-Suchard company (which operated from 1928 to 1959) described the process of bringing cocoa beans from the tree to the table:

The pods, when cut from the tree by knives on the end of long poles, are thrown together in heaps on the ground and allowed to remain a day or two. They are then split open and seeds, with the soft pulp, are taken out and placed in trenches in the ground or in wood vats and fermented for some days. The pulp liquefies and runs off while the beans are later dried in the air and sunlight. They are then placed in bags of from one hundred to two hundred and twenty five pounds each and are ready for shipment. These seeds are the cocoa beans of commerce.

When received by the manufacturers the beans are first carefully cleaned and picked, then roasted and rapidly cooled. The roasting decidedly alters the flavor of the bean, quite as much as roasting a potato. The roasted beans are then crushed in order to separate the shell. This is done by means of air blasts. The broken beans are known as Cocoa "Nibs". The nibs are next ground in friction mills, from which they come out as a thick, heavy fluid. The grinding has liberated the oil from the fibre cells, while the heat liquefies it, hence the result—known technically as "Chocolate Liquor". By mixing this liquor with sugar and flavor, regrinding, tempering in hot rooms and molding into cakes, chocolate for eating purposes is produced.

When the liquor is subjected to hydraulic pressure, a clear, limpid oil, which melts at a rather high temperature, is extracted. This is the "Cocoa Butter" of commerce. The solid portion of the chocolate liquor which remains is then powdered, sifted and boxed and is the cocoa powder for beverage use. (*The Story of the Cocoa Bean*, Wilbur-Suchard Chocolate Company, Lititz, Penna.)

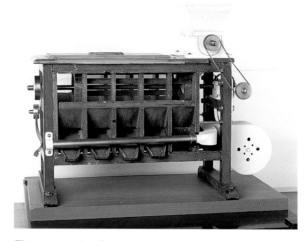

This is a cracker-fanner, used to remove the loosened shells from the cocoa beans and break the beans into "nibs."

These miniature versions of machinery used in chocolate manufacture illustrate some of the traditional steps involved. Shown first is a cocoa bean roaster, used for developing the flavor of the beans and loosening the shells for the next stage.

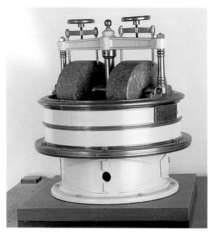

Melangeur, used for blending together chocolate liquor, sugar, milk, and cocoa butter.

Two stage grinder, used for refining the nibs into a thick liquid known in the industry as "chocolate liquor."

Three roll refiner, used for adding smoothness to chocolate coatings.

These glass cylinders illustrate the "before and after" process of chocolate manufacture. In the back are jars of cocoa beans, cocoa nibs (the inner part of the bean), and leftover cocoa shells. In the front are jars of chocolate drops made by subjecting the tiny nibs to high pressure and heat. Cocoa bean shells, though a waste product of the chocolate industry, are valued by the chemical and medical industries due to their high percentage of an alkaloid called theobromine.

Africa's Ivory Coast is the primary source of the world's cocoa bean harvest today, followed by such countries as Brazil and Malaysia. And where are the resulting delicacies ultimately consumed? The Swiss eat more chocolate than anyone else—approximately 22 pounds per person in 1998, according to the Chocolate Manufacturer's Association. Other chocolate loving countries include Germany, Belgium, Denmark, England, Ireland, and Austria, all of whose inhabitants consumed more than 17 pounds per person that same year. And the American public? Close on their heels, enjoying an average of 12.2 pounds per person—or more than 3 billion pounds in total!

Chocolate Molds

With their often charming depictions of animals and figures, metal chocolate molds have become highly sought acquisitions in today's antiques and collectible world. They were manufactured in both the United States and Europe starting around 1870 and reached the height of their popularity in the 1920s. Major names in the industry include several Létang firms in France; Herman Walter, Anton Reiche, and J.G. Laurosch in Germany; plus Eppelsheimer & Co. and the American Chocolate Mold Co. in the U.S.

Holiday themes were among the most common used for chocolate molds, along with animals of all types, nursery rhyme characters, airplanes, cars, and other vehicles—even historical events. Not surprisingly, molds often reflected images that were unique to individual countries' celebration of a particular holiday. Christmas molds, for example, could depict the "Jolly Santa familiar in the United States, [or] the fur-trimmed long-coated Father Christmas known in the European countries, while the Christmas mold that resembled a Bishop predominated in the Netherlands and Belgium." (Hanes, 1998, 38)

Chocolate molds were manufactured in a variety of styles, many of which are illustrated here. They can be one-sided or two-sided, with the two-sided molds either hinged or held together with various forms of clamps. Flat, one piece trays are also found, often with repeated figures and sometimes bearing the company name or logo. The durability of these metal molds was an advantage to chocolate manufacturers of the time and has obviously helped the molds survive throughout the years—to the delight of those who enjoy them today!

The value of chocolate molds depends largely on who the manufacturer was, the age of the mold, the subject matter (Christmas and Halloween molds are generally the most collectible), and the condition.

Metal mold for eight bars of chocolate, each embossed "Wilbur." 4" x 9". $35-65.

Large metal chocolate mold for "Wilbur's / Philadelphia." 6.5" x 4". $50-75.

Left and above:
Small metal molds for two squares of Suchard chocolate each, four with flat rim, 3.5" x 2.25", one without rim, 3.2" x 1.5". $5-10 ea.

Metal chocolate mold with "W S C" on each of
twelve rectangles. 7.75" x 4.5". $15-25.

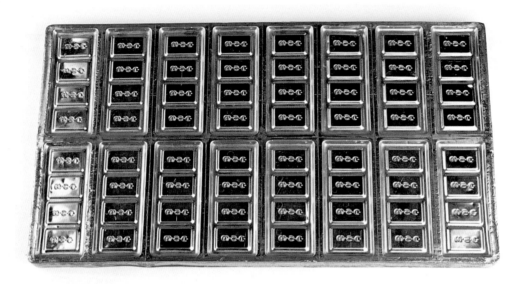

Larger metal chocolate mold, sixty-four individual rectangles with "W S C,"
marked American Chocolate Mold Company. 15.75" x 8.75". $25-45.

Detail of larger "W S C" mold.

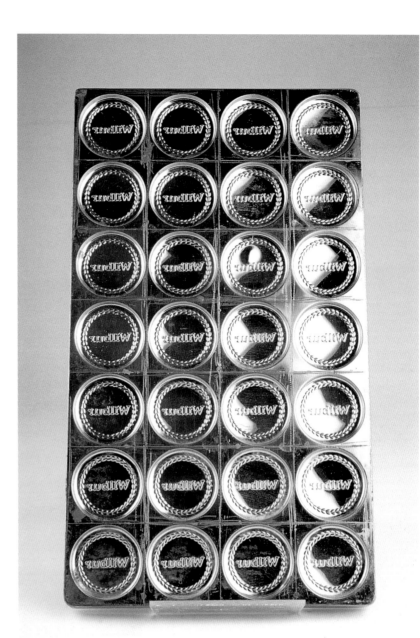

Metal chocolate mold, individual circles with "Wilbur" in the center, made by the American Chocolate Mold Company. 14.25" x 8.25". $30-60.

"The chocolate that was used for Bud stock, was made with the greatest care and was especially well ground. The nibs after the usual cleaning, were all picked over by hand to take out any bits of shell that had gotten by the fans. The finished paste was either moulded in blocks and put into storage or it was re-ground and put in the hot room for twenty-four hours or more. When it was finally ready for moulding, it was dropped from funnels. The individual Bud was rather jelly-like at this stage so the trays of Buds had to be put in the refrigerator by hand since any other conveyer would have shaken the form down and made the Buds lose their pleasing and characteristic shape with the flip on top." (from *Happy Days & Special Events of the Wilbur Family, 1898-1980*, compiled by Ross T. Wilbur, 1980)

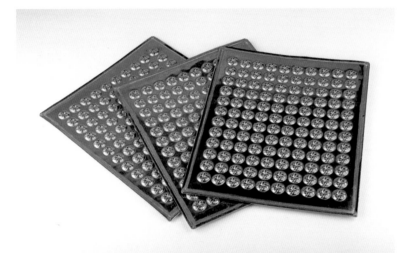

A trio of metal candy molds for the famous Wilbur Buds. 14" x 11.5", $25-35 ea.

Detail of Wilbur Buds molds.

Metal mold for eight souvenir medallions commemorating the 1926 Philadelphia Sesqui-Centennial, shown with four chocolate molded medallions. 4.5" x 8.75". $75-115.

Metal chocolate molds, two Victorian style Santas. Left: 7.25" x 3.5", marked "15554/ vormenfabriek Tilburg-Holland," $85-165. Right: 5.5" x 3", marked "167," $95-155.

Metal chocolate molds, three variations of Santa Claus. From left: 7" x 4.5", marked "8228," $25-40; 8" x 4.75", unmarked, $30-45; 6.25" x 4", marked "1/8050," $65-110.

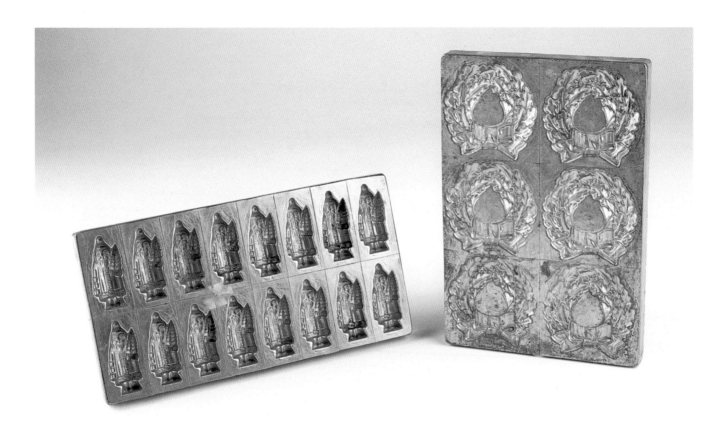

Two metal chocolate molds with holiday themes. Small Santas, 8.75" x 4.5", marked "5353/Van Emden Co., New York," $175-225; small wreaths, 8" x 5.5", marked "I.C. Weygandt Co., New York, Made in Germany/4708," $125-175.

Above and right:
Detail of the two holiday molds.

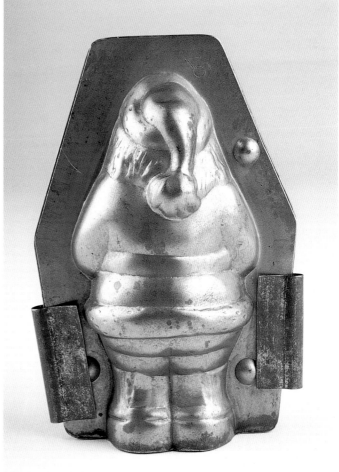

Above and right:
Metal chocolate mold, front and reverse of Santa Claus. 5" x 3.5", marked "46." $25-40.

Flat metal chocolate mold, small Santa heads, marked "4018/Made in Germany." 9.5" x 2.75". $175-200.

Metal chocolate mold, double Santas and reindeer. This mold was
probably made in Germany, c. 1930s. 10" x 4". $185-225.

Metal chocolate molds, two sizes and shapes of Easter rabbits. $40-90 ea.

Metal chocolate mold, Easter egg with rabbit. 5" x 3.5". $75-95.

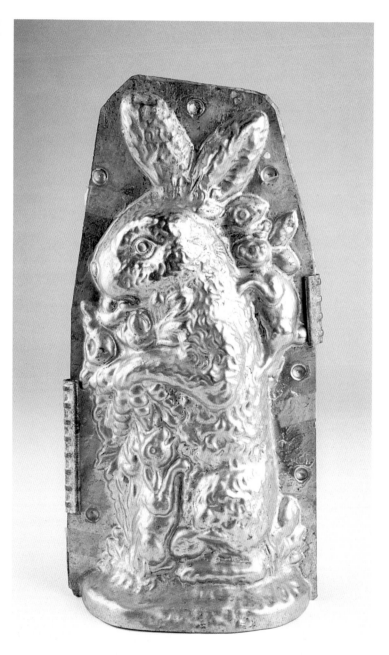

Metal chocolate mold, large rabbit with baby rabbits on back, made by New York manufacturer. 16.5" x 8". $425-550.

Metal chocolate molds, assorted sizes and shapes
of rabbits. From left: 6.25" x 5.5", marked "1 8177;"
3.25" x 3", marked "6626;" 9" x 6", unmarked; 7.5"
x 6.75", marked "460." $25-85 ea.

Metal chocolate molds, two sizes and shapes of baskets. Large
basket: 9" x 4.5". Small basket: 4.5" x 2". $25-65 ea.

Metal chocolate mold, rabbit with basket on back, marked "8197." 8.75" x 4.5". $50-75.

Metal chocolate mold, large Easter basket. 8.5" x 3.75". $45-65.

Two flat metal chocolate molds, one for twelve berries, the other for eighteen small rabbits sitting on eggs. 4" x 6" ea. Berries mold: $40-65. Rabbit with egg mold: $60-85.

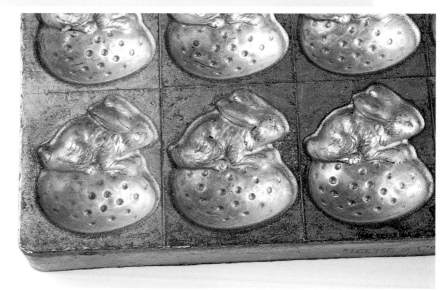

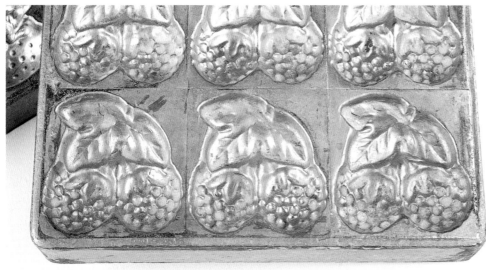

Left and above:
Detail of the berries and rabbit with egg molds.

Metal chocolate molds in various shapes. From left: rabbit, 4.75" x 3.75", marked "8157;" rabbit pulling cart, 5.25" x 3.75", unmarked; Easter elf riding rabbit, 4.25" x 5.25", marked "34 solid nickel silver, made in Germany." $35-195 ea.

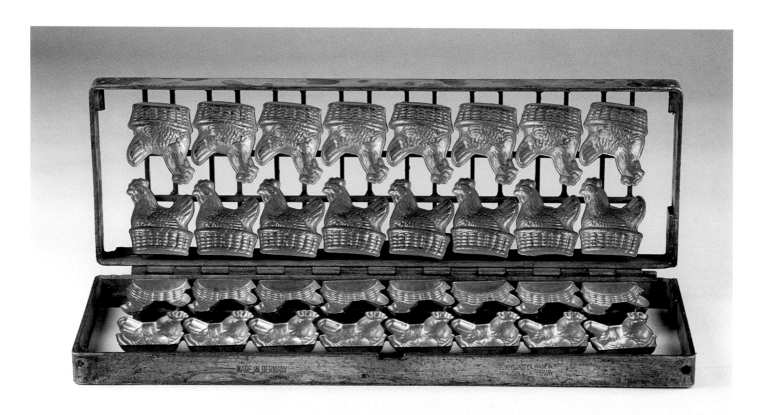

Hinged metal chocolate mold for sitting hens, made in Germany, c. 1930s. 16" x 11". $75-125.

Two metal chocolate molds, one in the shape of a duck, the other in the shape of a lamb. These molds are of more recent manufacture (after World War II). 5.5" h., $25-40 ea.

Metal chocolate molds, assorted sizes of children. From left: 5" x 4.5", marked "230076;" 7.5" x 3.5", marked "17507;" 5" x 3.5", marked "11"; 6.25" x 4", unmarked; 2.5" x 3.5", marked "175024." $65-125 ea.

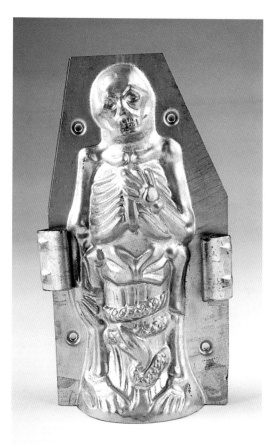

Metal chocolate mold in the shape of a skeleton, also of more recent manufacture. 5.5" h. $25-40.

Left and below:
Metal chocolate mold of smiling child, front and reverse, marked "17498," c. 1930s. 8" x 3.5". $165-195.

Hinged metal mold for five chocolate cigars. 4.5" x 5". $20-45.

Two metal chocolate molds, c. 1930s. Small girl with muff, marked "24114 / Made in Germany," and boy with book, marked "24113." 5" x 2.5" ea. $225-295 for pair.

Metal chocolate molds of two Dutch children, girl marked "17605/69," boy marked "24247 made in Dresden." 6" x 3.5" ea. $195-235 for pair.

Many additional chocolate molds, as well as a wonderful assortment of vintage cookware and utensils, can be seen in this replica of an early candy kitchen housed at the Wilbur Chocolate Company's Candy Americana Museum.

Chapter Three
Packaging—Boxes, Buds, Bars, and More

The rise of the chocolate industry at the end of the nineteenth century coincided with a rise in America's penchant for brand name, pre-packaged goods, especially food products. Prior to around 1880, many foods were sold in bulk form out of barrels, bins, or sacks, with little regard to who actually manufactured them. As pre-packaged foods became more popular, however, package design quickly assumed great importance.

Historian Daniel Boorstin has aptly noted that there is a subtle but significant distinction between "packing," intended to transport and preserve, and "packaging," intended to sell. (Boorstin, 1974, 435) As brand names became more and more the norm in America's early twentieth century marketplace, the ability of consumers to identify (and then buy) a product based on package recognition alone became paramount. Indeed, package design became a profession unto itself and designers studied the way such variables as shape, size, and color influenced purchasing decisions.

The first "chocolate box" is reported to have been introduced as early as 1868, when British confectioner Richard Cadbury used a painting of his own daughter and her kitten to decorate one of his candy boxes. Subsequent chocolate manufacturers would soon discover that package quality—as well as product quality—was necessary for a successful business. In its *1939 Year Book*, the Retail Confectioners' Association of Philadelphia, Inc. included an article on "Candy Merchandising," advising members that the "neatness, quality and general arrangement of the package itself is probably the best invitation to return for 'more of the same.' If a customer is proud to have your package on display in the home, that customer is likely to be an asset to your business, both through direct purchases, and through favorable publicity spread through a circle of friends." Ads from box companies can be found in the same publication: the Jesse Jones Paper Box Co. advertises "Candy Boxes Worthy of Their Contents," Henry Schmidt & Bro., Inc. note that "Schmidt Boxes Are Better Boxes," and still a third advertiser touts "Boxes That Do Credit to Your Product."

Wooden box, Wilbur's Premium Baking Chocolate. H.O. Wilbur &
Sons, Inc., Philadelphia, Pa. 10.5" x 7" x 6.5". $30-40.

Wooden box and lid for 6 lbs. of Wilbur's 5¢ Vanilla Sweet Chocolate with boar trademark on lid, H. O. Wilbur & Sons, Philadelphia. "From H. P. Wilson, Altoona, Pa." marked on front of box. 10.6" x 8.9" x 2.6". $25-45.

Small cigar box for chocolate cigars, top marked "El Cupido Cigars de Chocolate," front marked "H. O. Wilbur & Sons, Fabrica de Chocolate," sides marked "Colorado" on left and "Habana" on right. 5.25" x 3.25" x 1.25". $15-25.

Assorted wooden boxes for Ideal chocolate and cocoa products. Top left: Chocolate Biscuits box with lid, "1 cent each." Bottom left: Ideal Cocoa box, no lid. Right: Chocolate Mascots box with hinged lid, "1 cent each." $15-25 ea.

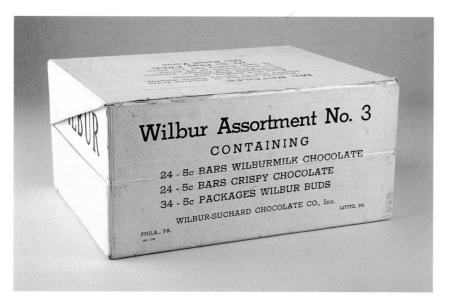

Above and right:
Display box for "Wilbur Assortment No. 3." Top of box provides hints to retailers as well as information regarding the inclusion of ten free 5¢ packages. Wilbur-Suchard Chocolate Co., Inc. Philadelphia and Lititz, Pa. 11" x 9" x 5.25". $25-35.

Large cardboard box marked "Wilbur Quality Chocolate." 10.75" x 4.75". $15-20.

Cardboard box with lid for twelve packages of Suchard Chocolate Squares, Mint.
Made by Wilbur-Suchard Chocolate Co., Inc. Lititz Penna., c. 1930s. $20-30.

Top: cardboard box for Wilbur's Chocolate Buds, with stirring cupid logo. 10.5" x 3.5".
Bottom: wooden box for 6 lbs. of Wilbur's Sweet Chocolate. 10" x 3". $20-25 ea.

Wilbur Buds, first sold in 1894, have gone through many packaging changes. Starting with these very early boxes, the photos that follow illustrate the variety of boxes and tins used for Buds through the years. These assorted size boxes all have the stirring cupid logo on the front and are from H.O. Wilbur & Sons, Inc., Philadelphia, Pa. Height range: 4.25" to 6.5". $25-45 ea.

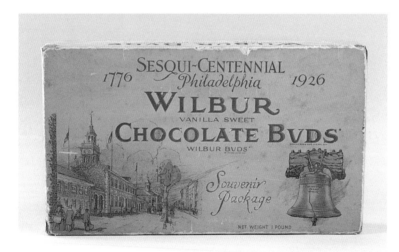

Souvenir package for Wilbur Chocolate Buds, made for the Sesqui-Centennial, 1776-1926, Philadelphia. 8.25" x 4.75". $35-50.

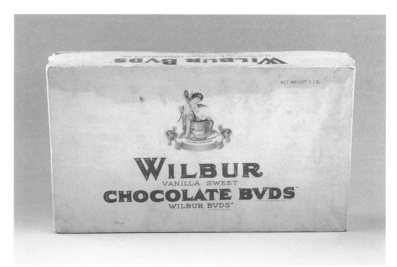

This white box with the stirring cupid logo in color was for 1 lb. of Wilbur Vanilla Sweet Chocolate Buds, 8.25" x 4.75". $15-20.

Wilbur's Buds tin, 2 lbs., gold with pink and blue stirring cupid logo. This is a replica of one originally made for H. O. Wilbur and Sons, Inc., Philadelphia, Pa. Bottom of tin marked "TINDECO." 7" dia. $25-35.

Detail of lid from the Wilbur's Buds tin, showing the stirring cupid logo.

Two 1 lb. boxes of Wilbur Buds, red with foil wrapped bud design. 8.25" x 4.75", $30-45 ea.

Side of red Buds box, with stirring cupid logo.

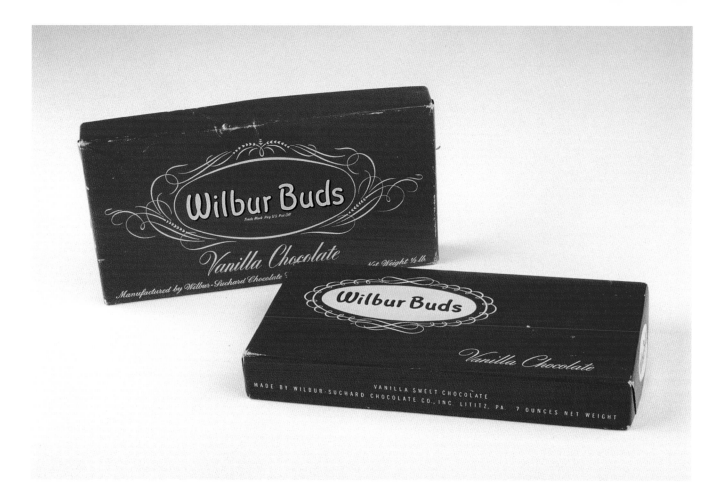

Pair of Wilbur Buds boxes, Wilbur-Suchard
Chocolate Co. Inc., Lititz, Pa. 8" x 4", $30-45 ea.

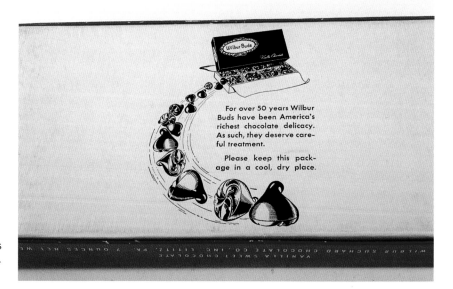

Bottom of the upper box, with Buds
illustration and storage instructions.

Cellophane wrapper for 2/3 oz. of Wilbur Buds, "Let
One Melt in Your Mouth." 6.25" x 2.4". $15-20.

Three 7 oz. boxes of Wilbur Buds,
c. 1950s. 8.25" x 4", $30-40 ea.

Wilbur Buds box, 7 oz. of "New Continental
Milk Chocolate." 8.25" x 4". $10-15.

Wilbur's Milk Chocolate Buds and Wilbur's Dark
Sweet Chocolate Buds, 5.5 oz. boxes, Wilbur
Chocolate Company, Lititz, Pa. 8.25" x 4", $15-20 ea.

Pair of Wilbur Buds boxes, yellow rose design and
"Famous since 1884" on front. 8" x 4", $10-15 ea.

Two 5.5 oz. boxes of Wilbur Buds, Mint Flavored Semisweet
Chocolate and Original Dark Sweet Chocolate. 8" x 4", $10-15 ea.

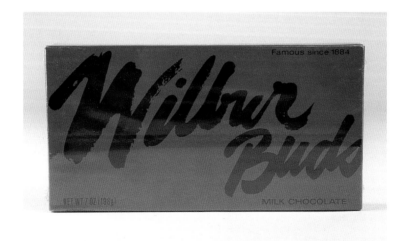

Wilbur Buds box, 7 oz., with large, contemporary style writing and
"Famous since 1884" in corner. $10-15.

Left and below:
Round metal tin for Wilbur's Chocolate Buds. A replica of the original from H.O. Wilbur & Sons, this one was made by the present day Wilbur Chocolate Co., Inc., Lititz, Pa. 6.5" dia.

These red and green square boxes held round metal tins of Wilbur's Chocolate Buds. They were sold through the early 1990s.

Four contemporary boxes of Wilbur's Buds in assorted flavors, each box with a different color striped design, 5.5 oz. each. Wilbur Chocolate Co., Inc., Lititz, Pa. 4" x 8" ea.

Box of Wilbur Buds packaged exclusively for the Candy Americana Museum and Factory Candy Outlet, Wilbur Chocolate Co., Lititz, Pa. 6.5" h.

Noah's Ark Ideal Milk Chocolate Animals box, 1 3/4 oz., with story of Noah's Ark on reverse, Brewster-Ideal Chocolate Co. Lititz, Pa. Note handles formed from elephants' trunks. 4.5" x 3.5". $60-90.

Another, probably later, version of Ideal Milk Chocolate Animals, made by the Ideal Cocoa and Chocolate Company, Lititz, Pa. $35-50.

Two paper boxes from the Wilbur-Suchard Chocolate Co., Lititz, Pa. Black box and lid, 5.25" x 3.5"; round purple box and lid, 4" dia. $15-20 ea.

Above and left:
These cardboard boxes folded to resemble buildings were part of the Suchard Chocolate Village made by the Wilbur-Suchard Chocolate Co., Inc., Lititz, Pa. 3.5" x 4", $10-15 ea.

Large box of Wilbur's Milk Chocolate with Almonds. This 5 lb. box was discontinued in the mid-1980s. 18" x 10". $10-15.

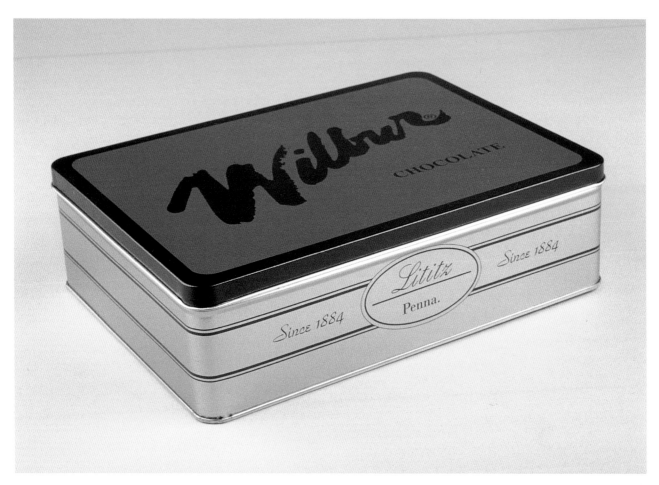

Here are two examples of contemporary Wilbur packaging. The metal tin has a gold and brown design and measures 6.5" x 9". The wooden lock corner boxes come in brown or green and are used to send present day Wilbur products via mail order. 7.25" x 10.5".

Candy Bars and Wrappers

Candy bars come in many different varieties, of course, but the most popular by far are those made of chocolate (or at least chocolate covered!). The individually wrapped candy bar as we know it today, however—complete with colorful, enticing label—was not a staple of the marketplace until the early part of the twentieth century. Prior to that time, chocolate and other types of candy were generally sold loose by the pound, half pound, or so on, rather than just a few pieces at a time. As machinery became available for wrapping, however, all that changed. The same process used from around 1911 on for wrapping bars of soap was easily adapted to wrapping bars of chocolate, and soon these convenient and tempting little packages were showing up on the shelves of drugstores, newsstands, and grocery stores everywhere. (Divone, 1987, 30)

The popularity of candy bars really took off after World War I, and the going price at that time dropped from around 10 cents to 5 cents. During the Depression years, it was not uncommon to find candy bars selling for just a penny. And no price can be put on the eminent value of candy bars to U.S. servicemen and women from both world wars through the Gulf War of 1990—they have not only been a source of extra energy in ration kits, they have "allowed G.I. Joe to form friendships with those whose language he couldn't speak." (Broekel, 1882, 12)

Paper wrapper for 1-3/4 oz. bar of Wilbur's 5¢ Sweet Clover Chocolate, color lithography with stirring cupid logo. 2.9" x 5.4" folded. $75-100.

This framed jigsaw puzzle boasts a collage of colorful candy bars, some of which have become American institutions through the years.

54

3 oz. bar of Wilbur 5¢ Sweet Chocolate with Roasted Peanuts. Note variation of stirring cupid logo on front. 8" x 3.75". $25-35.

Top: 6 oz. bar of Wilbur Clover Milk Chocolate, 7.5" x 4.25". Bottom: 4 oz. bar of Wilbur Sweet Chocolate with Roasted Peanuts, 8" x 4". The company name is hard to miss on these two candy bars! $15-20 ea.

3/4 oz. bar of Wilbur Sweet Chocolate with Toasted Peanuts, 4.5" x 1.5". $15-20.

Elegantly designed paper wrapper for 1/2 pound of Ideal Almond Chocolate, made by the Ideal Cocoa & Chocolate Co. 10.5" x 9". $15-20.

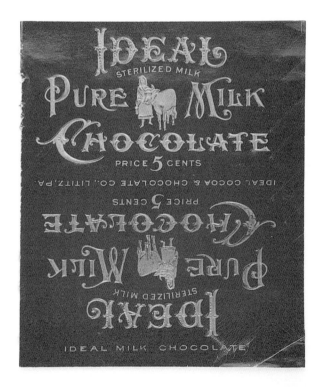

Gold embossed paper wrapper for Ideal Pure Milk Chocolate, Ideal Cocoa & Chocolate Co., Lititz, Pa. 5.5" x 6.25". $30-40.

Paper wrapper for Ideal Penny Sweet Chocolate, "The Original 5¢ Almond Bar," Ideal Cocoa and Chocolate Co., Lititz, Pa. $30-40.

Paper wrapper for 1/2 pound of Ideal Unsweetened Chocolate, Ideal Cocoa and Chocolate Co. 11" x 8.5". $15-25.

Three paper wrappers for Suchard bars made by the Wilbur-Suchard Chocolate Co.: #2847, Milk Chocolate; #2852, Milk Chocolate Crisp; and #2851, Milk Chocolate with Almonds. $10-15 ea.

Large cellophane wrapper for 24 - 5¢ Milk Chocolate Bars, Wilbur-Suchard Chocolate Co. Inc., Lititz, Penna. 14.75" x 22". $10-15.

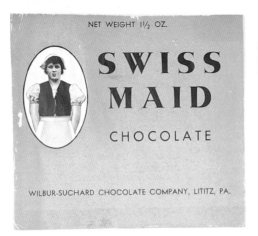

Two paper wrappers from the Wilbur-Suchard Chocolate Co., one for 1-1/2 oz. bar of Swiss Maid chocolate, 5" x 4.5", the other for 1 oz. bar of Suchard Bittra, 3.3" x 4.75". $15-20 ea.

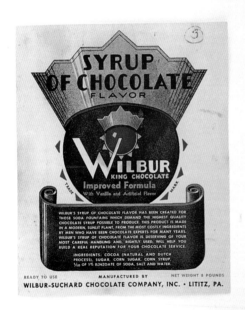

Paper label for 8 pound container holding "Syrup of Chocolate Flavor," Wilbur-Suchard Chocolate Company, Lititz, Pa. 4" x 5". $20-25.

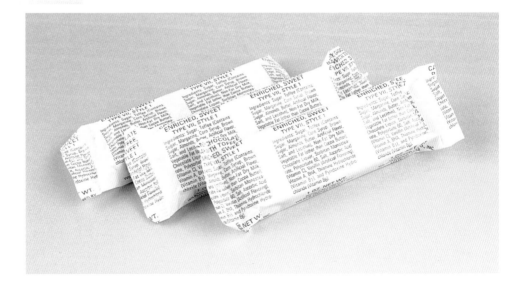

Ration bars made by the Wilbur-Suchard Chocolate Co. for U. S. soldiers in World War II. "Candy, Chocolate Bar with Toffee, Enriched, Sweet, Type VII, Style 1." 4" x 1" ea. $15 ea.

8 oz. package of Wilbur Baking Chocolate, Wilbur Chocolate Co., Lititz, Pa. 6.5" x 3.5". $20-25.

2.5 oz. Muhammad Ali® Crisp Crunch Bar, made by the Wilbur Chocolate Co., Lititz, Pa., c. late 1970s. These bars were produced for approximately six months only, after Wilbur was approached by Muhammad Ali's promoters to create a candy bar with his image. Ali himself toured the factory in 1978 and met with the workers and Lititz residents. $35-45.

Four 3 oz. bars of Wilbur chocolate in assorted flavors, made by the Wilbur Chocolate Co., c. 1980s. 6.5" x 2", $10 ea.

Two 3 oz. bars of Wilbur Gourmet
Baking Chocolate, made by the Wilbur
Chocolate Co., c. 1980s. 6" x 2", $10 ea.

Wilbur Centennial Chocolate Collection from 1984, boxed set of
three different 4 oz. bars commemorating the Wilbur Chocolate
Company's 100th anniversary. $15-25.

Bottom of Centennial Chocolate Collection box, with description of each flavor.

Left and below left:
Assorted bars of Wilbur's chocolate, all 2.5 oz. except Milk Chocolate Crisp (2.25 oz.), made by the Wilbur Chocolate Co. These bars were discontinued in the early 1990s.

Box of four Wilbur's Chocolate bars in assorted flavors, 2.25 oz. each, made by the Wilbur Chocolate Co., Lititz, Pa.

Box of four Wilbur chocolate bars made without sugar, 2.5 oz. each. Includes Milk Chocolate, Milk Chocolate with Almonds, Dark Chocolate, Milk Chocolate with Almonds. Gold cover decorated with "I Love Wilbur Chocolate" teddy bear.

Two extra large bars of Wilbur's Milk Chocolate with Almonds, 5 lb. and 2 lb. sizes, made by the Wilbur Chocolate Co., Inc., Lititz, Pa.

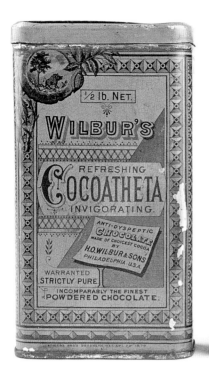

Two 1/2 pound canisters of Wilbur's Refreshing Cocoa-Theta, one of the earliest chocolate products made by H. O. Wilbur & Sons. Canister with lid, printed tin; canister without lid, paper label over tin. 2.75" x 5", $35-45 ea.

Cocoa Tins and Jars

Cocoa for drinking or baking is the result of extracting cocoa butter from ground up cacao beans, leaving behind a pressed "cake" of chocolate that is then cooled, pulverized, and sifted. Not all of the cocoa butter is removed, however; in the early years of manufacture much prepared cocoa still had an oily film on top created by the remaining cocoa butter. This either had to be skimmed off the top or "soaked up" through the addition of starch to the cocoa. Today's cocoa may have 10% or more cocoa butter content, and the slightly richer "Breakfast Cocoa" must contain at least 22% cocoa butter. Dutch process cocoa, which has been treated with an alkali, has a slightly milder flavor and darker appearance than regular cocoa.

One of the earliest products sold by H.O. Wilbur & Sons was "Coco-Theta," marketed as a nourishing product for sick or ailing individuals. In a c. 1890 description of this product, the company noted that it is

[the] choicest product of the Cocoa Bean. Highly nutritious and extremely palatable. It forms a delightful beverage for all. It is the only preparation of powdered chocolate adapted to the use of dyspeptics, while for children and aged it is invaluable. Put up in 1-lb. and 1/2-lb. tins, and sold by the best trade everywhere. Ask for it.

Testimonials on the side of one Cocoa-Theta tin.

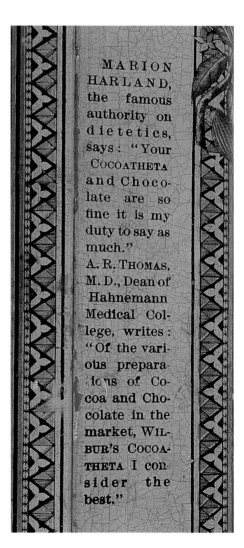

MARION HARLAND, the famous authority on dietetics, says: "Your COCOATHETA and Chocolate are so fine it is my duty to say as much." A. R. THOMAS, M. D., Dean of Hahnemann Medical College, writes: "Of the various preparations of Cocoa and Chocolate in the market, WILBUR'S COCOA-THETA I consider the best."

Some years later, the Wilbur-Suchard company distributed a series of "tried and tested" recipes using cocoa, including recipes for standard drinking cocoa as well as cocoa syrup, cocoa drop biscuits, cocoa sandwiches ("takes the place of cake"), and cocoa bread pudding. The company prefaced the recipes with a persuasive description of "Why You Should Use Cocoa," including among other reasons that:

Cocoa nourishes and strengthens the body by building real muscle and sinew. It refreshes the system, mildly stimulates the brain, quiets the nerves. It is easily digested and supplies great sustenance in compact form. For this reason, the United States Government keeps her soldiers and sailors liberally supplied. For the same reason, its use is highly beneficial, not only to all those engaged in prolonged physical effort such as travelers, explorers and outdoor men generally, but also to those engaged in pursuits where mental concentration is required.

As can be seen in the following photographs, tin boxes have been the most favored type of packaging for cocoa (and a favorite of collectors for their colorful graphics, as well). The tightly covered tins helped maintain the freshness and flavor of the cocoa inside; one especially watertight cocoa tin is reported to have been tossed from a sinking ship in 1933 bearing a note inside, only to turn up on a beach in Wales years later—note intact! (Fleming, 1998, 50)

Two early cocoa tins, one with paper label and stirring cupid logo, the other with "H.O. Wilbur & Sons, Inc. / Breakfast Cocoa / Philadelphia" embossed on lid. 4.25" high ea. Left: $50-60. Right: $15-20.

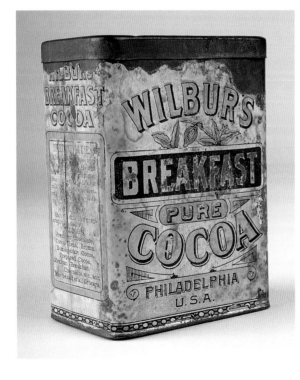

Wilbur's Breakfast Cocoa tin, H.O. Wilbur & Sons, Inc., Philadelphia, Pa. 4.25" high. $20-25. Detail from reverse of tin shown above.

Wilbur's Breakfast Cocoa in three different size tins, H.O. Wilbur & Sons,
Inc., Philadelphia, Pa. The two smaller tins may be salesmen's samples.
From left: 3.25" high, $100-150; 6" high, $25-35; 3.25" high, $100-150.

Three cylindrical cocoa tins. From left: Wilbur's Breakfast Cocoa,
3.5" high, $40-50; Wilbur's Cocoa with "10¢" and stirring cupid logo
on front, 3.5" high, $40-50; Nelson Cocoa, made by H.O. Wilbur &
Sons, Philadelphia, Pa., 3.5" high, $15-20.

Two Wilbur-dutch Cocoa tins, blue with stirring cupid logo on front, H.O. Wilbur & Sons Inc., Philadelphia, Pa. 12 oz. tin, 6" high; 8 oz. tin, 4" high. $25-35 ea.

Ideal Breakfast Cocoa tins, "Absolutely Pure and Soluble," made by the Kendig Chocolate Co., Lititz, Pa. Left: 4.25" high; right: 3.5" high. $45-55 ea.

Assortment of cocoa tins in different sizes and with different labels, all from the Ideal Cocoa & Chocolate Co., Lititz, Pa. Average height: 4". $25-35 ea.

Assortment of cocoa tins for Ideal Cocoa and Breakfast Cocoa, Ideal Cocoa & Chocolate Co., Lititz, Pa. The smallest tin in the center is 2.5" high and was a salesman's sample. Sample tin: $60-90. All others: $30-40 ea.

Assortment of cocoa tins from different companies, all part of the Wilbur "family." From left: Ideal Cocoa in 1 lb. and 1/2 lb. tins, Wilbur-Suchard Chocolate Co., Inc.; Ideal Cocoa in 1 lb. tin, Brewster-Ideal Chocolate Co.; Ideal Breakfast Cocoa and Ideal Cocoa, Ideal Cocoa & Chocolate Co. $30-40 ea.

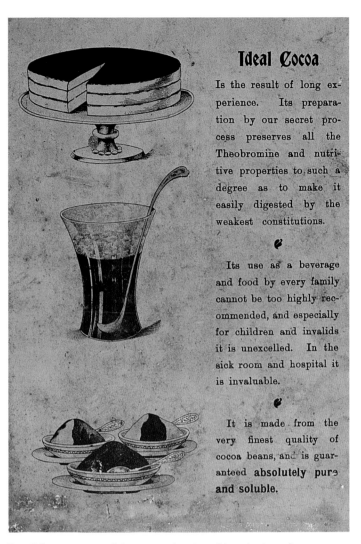

Detail from reverse of the cocoa tin, describing the benefits of drinking cocoa and the quality of the product.

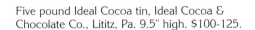

Five pound Ideal Cocoa tin, Ideal Cocoa & Chocolate Co., Lititz, Pa. 9.5" high. $100-125.

Superior Cocoa round tin, Ideal Cocoa & Chocolate Co., Lititz, Pa. 7" high. $45-55.

Left and below:
Glass jar for Ideal Milk Cocoa, Ideal Cocoa & Chocolate Co., with preparation instructions on the side. 5.5" high. $20-30.

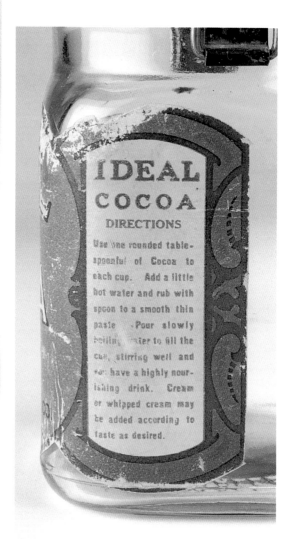

One pound tins of Wilbur's Breakfast Cocoa, each with stirring cupid logo. Left and right tins made by Wilbur-Suchard Chocolate Co., Inc., center tin made by Wilbur Chocolate Co., Inc. Note "Good Housekeeping Seal of Approval" on right hand tin. 7" high, $30-40 ea.

Below and right:
Wilbur 20 Second Instant Chocolate Flavor tin, with serving instructions for hot and cold on reverse, half pound size, Wilbur-Suchard Chocolate Company, Inc., Lititz, Pa. 4.5" high. $10-15.

Wantsmor Cocoa box, 1 lb., with mixing directions in six different languages on side of box, Wilbur-Suchard Chocolate Co., Philadelphia and Lititz, Pa. 7.25" high. $75-100.

Ideal Cocoa tins, all "Dutch Process," Wilbur Chocolate
Co., Lititz, Pa. Two 8 oz. tins, marked #403, 4.5" high
each; 16 oz. tin, marked #400, 6" high. $10 ea.

These two contemporary cocoa tins are from the Wilbur Chocolate
Co., Inc. Each features Wilbur's historic stirring cupid logo.

Chapter Four

Advertising and Promotion— Getting the Word Out

Although chocolate is so universally appealing one might think that it would "sell itself," manufacturers of chocolate have historically needed to convince prospective consumers not only to buy chocolate in general, but to buy *their* brand in particular. Advertising, of course, is the means by which this is done, and the words and pictures employed in the process afford us a fascinating look at chocolate's image through the years.

All advertising must first get our attention, then convince us that what is being sold is worthy of our hard earned dollars. Advertisers and merchandisers have many avenues from which to choose, though advertising has naturally had to keep pace with historical developments in mass media. Before newspapers and magazines were widely available, for example, merchants relied on signs, posters, and handbills to get their name in front of the public. The late nineteenth century saw the advent of many early magazines, whose national circulation allowed advertisers to reach a far wider audience than ever before. As might be expected, the influence of magazine advertising has not diminished through the years. In fact, notes author Linda Fuller, current figures show that when a magazine has chocolate on the cover, sales are likely to double! (Fuller, 1994, 3)

Images of women and children were widely used in early advertising, as will be seen in many of the examples that follow. During the early part of the 1900s, women were seen as the primary decision makers when it came to purchasing goods; by the Depression years " 'the American wife and mother' were perceived as advertising's primary market." (Goodrum and Dalrymple, 1990, 39) Portraying women in advertising was obviously seen as a way for them to relate to the product being offered, making it more likely they would buy it as a result. And an adorable child—no different than today—creates a pleasing image and positive association that makes just about any product more desirable.

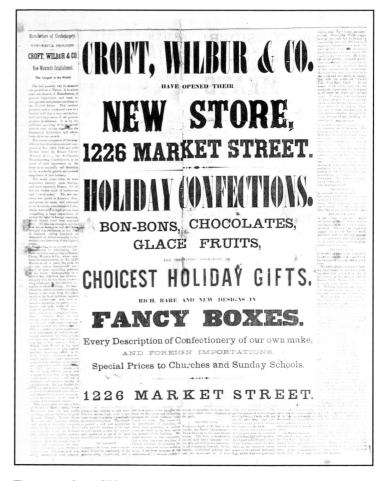

This copy of an 1878 newspaper advertisement and story announces the opening of a new store for Croft, Wilbur & Co. at 1226 Market Street in Philadelphia. $35-45.

Chocolate as Health Food: Remedy or Sweet Fantasy?

Today we think of chocolate far more as an indulgence than a curative, yet for many years this tasty treat was thought to provide medicinal qualities along with its obvious pleasurable qualities. Cortez and the early explorers observed how drinking chocolate seemed to afford the Aztecs great strength and fortitude; as noted in a 1926 description of chocolate's origins, "during the time of the festivities the Aztecs would spend all day and the greater part of the night in dancing with only cacao for nourishment, demonstrating conclusively the wonderful sustaining properties of chocolate." (*The Story of Chocolate and Cocoa*, 1926, 12)

As chocolate's popularity spread throughout Europe in the seventeenth and eighteenth centuries, it was often viewed as a potent remedy for chronic illness, poor digestion, even the proverbial broken heart. Not surprisingly, these putative therapeutic powers of chocolate show up as an advertising theme well into the nineteenth and even twentieth centuries—what better way to justify the enjoyment obtained from chocolate than by touting its ability to improve health?

Back in 1870, for example, one cocoa manufacturer boldly advised "pale people" that "from the above facts you will understand why persons who are pale, 'run down,' or recovering from illness, are greatly benefited by Runkel's Cocoa." Such individuals, Runkel's advised, "should drink one cupful of Runkel's every day at eleven and one at four o'clock as well as with their meals." (Fuller, 1994, 59).

Chocolate manufacturers were also fond of comparing chocolate's nutrient value to that of other foods, sometimes using expert testimonials to bolster their arguments. The inside front cover of Hershey's 1926 booklet about chocolate, for example, notes that "Bernarr Macfadden, Editor of the Physical Culture Magazine, says pure chocolate is a complete and concentrated food." Moreover, the article states, "[an] analysis indicates that a quarter pound of sweet milk chocolate has more nutritive material in it than a quart of milk and nearly as much as a dozen of eggs." (The company cautioned, however, that this analysis was intended to illustrate in an "emphatic manner" the nourishing value of chocolate and did not "necessarily indicate the advisability of eating chocolate instead of milk and eggs.")

Food comparisons were also used by the Wilbur-Suchard Chocolate Company, whose article about the cocoa bean acknowledged the dual nature of chocolate's appeal. "Most people who use chocolate use it as they would candy, simply because they like it . . ." begins one paragraph. "The fact is," continues the article, "that cocoa for drinking or baking and chocolate for eating are valuable foods. Analysis shows that cocoa and chocolate contain proteids [sic], like the nourishing part of bread and beef; starch, like potatoes and baked beans; fat, like the fat of meats and butter; and a gentle tonic similar to the active principle of tea and coffee but without their harmful effects. In reality, a cake of chocolate is a kind of concentrated and combined full meal . . ."

Though we may raise our eyebrows a bit at these assertions, the fact is that cocoa beans do contain the alkaloid called theobromine, which is used medicinally as both a stimulant and a diuretic. And the "healthy" aspects of chocolate continue to be discussed, debated, and researched today: a search of the Internet for this book turned up notice that recent studies at the University of Scranton indicate chocolate may contain the same kind of antioxidants found in fruits, vegetables, and red wine. Chocolate as health food? Perhaps . . .!

Framed advertisement for H.O. Wilbur & Sons with illustration of mother and
three children holding cup of cocoa and cocoa tins. 7.5" x 11". $100-125.

Framed advertisement with little girl in cap, "Wilbur's Cocoa Builds Healthy Happy Children." 24" x 13.5". $175-200.

Newspaper advertisement for Wilbur's Cocoa from the New York *Mail and Express*, Christmas, 1898. Note reference to the company's logo, introduced about ten years previously: "Insist upon the package with the cupid on the label." 5.4" x 5.8". $15-25.

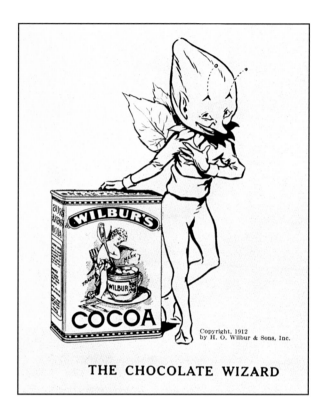

THE CHOCOLATE WIZARD

An elf like "Chocolate Wizard," whose head and wings seem to resemble a cocoa pod and leaves, appears in this 1912 ad for Wilbur's Cocoa. $10-15.

Oh!—I Forgot—!

Startling discovery of a little girl who purchased everything her mother told her to but finds that she has forgotten Wilbur's Cocoa.

Note—Always remember Wilbur's Cocoa as a food drink that is pure and nourishing, and entirely free from harmful stimulants or substitutes of any kind. Remember the name.

© 1919. By H. O. WILBUR & SONS, INC., Phila., Pa.

Black and white advertisement for Wilbur's Cocoa with little girl and big dog, "Oh—I Forgot—!" © H.O. Wilbur & Sons, Inc., Phila. Pa. $15-25.

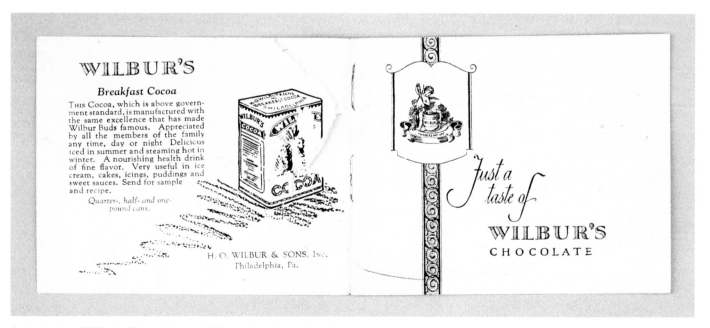

Just a taste of Wilbur's Chocolate, small 8-page brochure advertising products made by H.O. Wilbur & Sons. 3.5" x 2.75". $10-20.

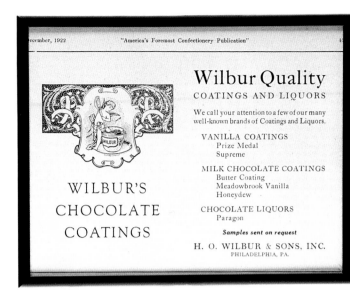

Trade journal advertisement for Wilbur's Chocolate Coatings made by H.O. Wilbur & Sons, Inc., c. 1922. 8" x 6". $15-20.

Right and below:
Advertising brochure for Cocoa-Theta from H.O. Wilbur & Sons, color lithographed front cover of stirring cupid and reference to Wilbur's receipt of the "highest award at Paris 1889" on back cover. Inside contains a printed letter entitled "Chocolate as she is ate" to Laura from Mary. 5.5" x 3.5". $15-25.

"Chocolate as she is ate"

MY DEAR LAURA:

I fancy I see a puzzled expression cross your face as you read the above lines and you wonder whether Mary has suddenly gone "daft"—but it is only the melancholy effect of an afternoon's study of "English as she is spoke."

I was so sorry you were unable to be at the reception last week. We had a delightful time—but the next morning—you know how it is—the music, the flowers, the lights, seem to be whirling through one's brain, and it requires quite an effort to "brace up" and "doe ye next thyngge," which, in my case, was to visit Perkins the grocer, and do the family marketing.

While making my purchases at Perkins', I looked longingly at the packages of Wilbur's sweet chocolate so temptingly displayed; and the salesman, knowing I seldom fail to include them, and being aware of my preferences, said, "Which will you have to-day, Miss Jenny, Wilbur's Imperial, or the Sweet Clover?" I replied quickly, remembering "He who hesitates is lost," "Neither, thank you, I'm afraid they're a little too rich for me, the way I feel."

Just then I caught sight of a blue-labeled tin marked simply with the word "COCOA-THETA."

"That is Wilbur's specialty," said the salesman. "It is the most wholesome preparation of Chocolate ever made by any manufacturer. Even a confirmed dyspeptic can enjoy it and not suffer any uncomfortable effects. You will find it stimulating and nutritious, and a delightful substitute for tea and coffee. There is less sugar in it than used in most chocolate, which makes it more digestible; and it is ready for instant use." He seemed ready to go on in this strain

indefinitely, but I interrupted him by ordering four packages.

I found the flavor entirely different from anything I had ever tasted in the way of chocolate, and am better pleased with it every day. I find I can drink it at any hour, or in any condition of health, and it bears out in every respect the words spoken for it by Perkins' clerk.

One package I gave to Auntie, who you know is very nervous and under treatment for indigestion. She felt so doubtful about it, afraid it wouldn't agree with her, she hadn't tasted chocolate for years, her doctor would be sure to disapprove—that I went down to her kitchen, and made it into a drink for her, using one spoonful to a cup of milk and water, and boiling one minute. I induced her to try it, and when I went away she was looking and feeling brighter than I had seen her for a long time. I called the next day to learn whether she had suffered any ill effects from the "COCOA-THETA," and found her doctor had ordered that it be given her regularly, that he considered it nourishing and stimulating, and the use of it would benefit her. She has since been buying of Colter.

Next I tried it on Tom, who called that evening. Tom, you know, is pretty slow about adopting anything new. "Mame, this is good. When we * * *" I think I will not repeat any more of the conversation!

I just notice that I haven't said much in this letter, except about "COCOA-THETA;" but I feel so enthusiastic about this new chocolate that I feel as if I must tell everybody. That you may try it for yourself, I send you by express a six-pound box with my compliments. Very sincerely yours, MARY.

P. S.—COCOA-THETA is for sale in Cincinnati by COLTER & CO., J. J. PERKINS & CO., and other fine grocers.

These small black and white advertisements for Wilbur Buds all date from the early 1900s and appeared in such magazines as *Women's Home Companion, McClure's,* and *Red Book*. Advertisers knew by this time that it was important to show the package, as well as the product, in order to build brand name recognition. $10-15 ea.

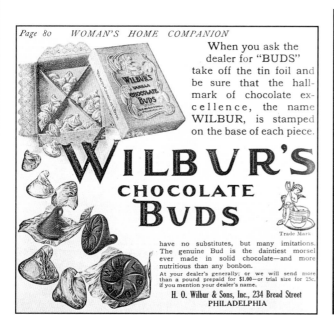

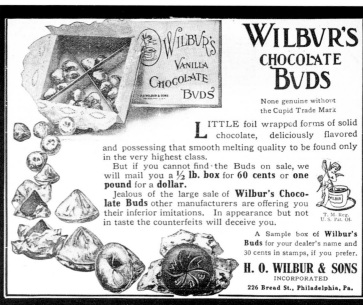

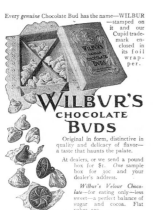

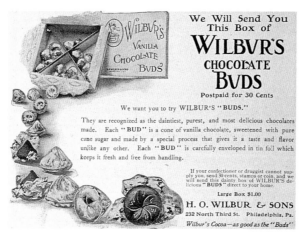

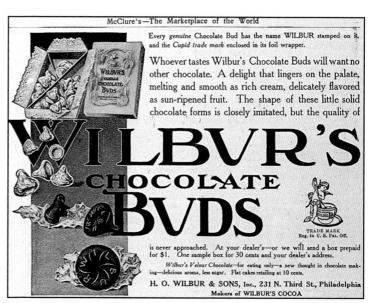

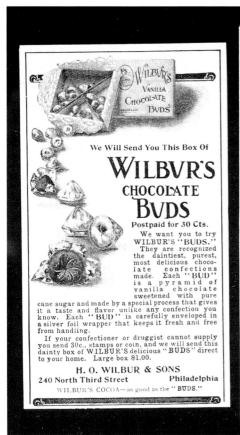
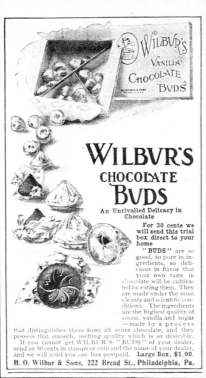
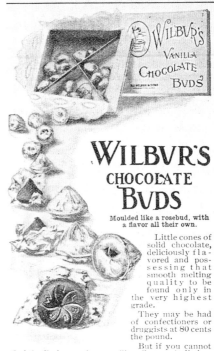

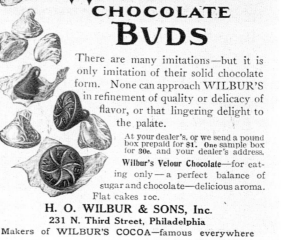

More ads for Wilbur Buds, these all featuring small children.
The use of endearing tots to promote products of all kinds is an
advertising technique still well entrenched today. $10-15 ea.

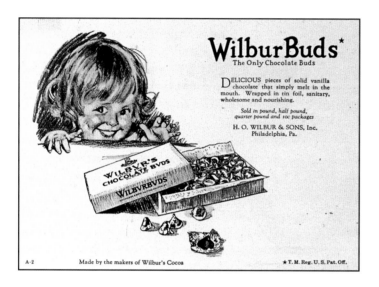

WilburBuds*

The Only Chocolate Buds

JUST the ideal Chocolate for the youngsters,— yet loved by the old folks, too.

These delicious morsels of solid vanilla Chocolate,— tin foil wrapped, are of the highest grade,— nourishing and satisfying. So there's no need to worry about how many they eat. Remember the name,— it is your safeguard.

Sold in pound, half pound,
quarter pound and 10c packages

Made by the makers of Wilbur's Cocoa

H. O. WILBUR & SONS, Inc.
Philadelphia, Pa.

★T. M. Reg. U. S. Pat. Off.   A-15

★T. M. Reg. U. S. Pat. Off.

WilburBuds*

The Only Chocolate Buds

These Vacation Days

DON'T forget the kiddies,— let them satisfy their chocolate hunger with Wilbur Buds. These delicious morsels of solid vanilla chocolate are pure and nourishing. Let them eat plenty.

Sold in pound, half pound,
quarter pound and 10c packages

H. O. WILBUR & SONS, Inc.
Philadelphia, Pa.

A-4

WILBVR'S
CHOCOLATE
BVDS

Too well known to need an introduction. The best cocoa, the finest
sugar and richest vanilla that can
be bought have made these Buds
perfect for a generation.
The formula has never been
changed.
Wilburbuds are the only genuine
Chocolate Buds. "Made to melt
in the mouth."

*Wrapped in pure tinfoil; put up
in 1 lb., 1-2 lb. and smaller
size fancy packages*

WILBVR'S
VELOVR
CHOCOLATE

For those who desire a
Swiss style Chocolate of
superior flavor and qual-
ity; smooth as velvet,
melting and satisfying. A
subtle flavor adds zest to
this blend of cocoa, va-
nilla and sugar.

Flat cakes only

WILBVR'S
DESSERT
CHOCOLATE

A bitter sweet Chocolate for
after dinner, when ordinary
chocolate is cloying.
CHOCOLATE LEAVES of nat-
ural dark chocolate, a little bitter;
pleasantly sweet; altogether delightful. According to medical author-
ities, chocolate aids digestion.

*In 1-2 lb. fancy packages
packed in layers*

WILBVR'S
BAKING
CHOCOLATE

Made of a selected blend of
rich cocoa beans, containing all the full food values
of chocolate.

This product is free from added
starch or any adulterant and is
of especial value for icings, pud-
dings, sauces and general house-
hold use — scientific roasting and
milling give the fine flavor and
excellent quality found only in
Wilbur's.

*Put up in 1 2-lb., 1 4-lb. and
1 5-lb. cartons.*

WILBVR'S CHOCOLATE AND COCOA PRODUCTS OF EXCELLENCE

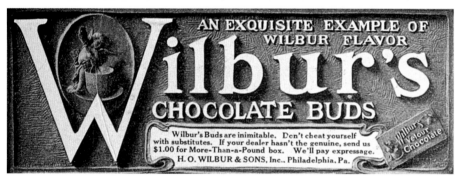

AN EXQUISITE EXAMPLE OF
WILBUR FLAVOR

Wilbur's
CHOCOLATE BUDS

Wilbur's Buds are inimitable. Don't cheat yourself
with substitutes. If your dealer hasn't the genuine, send us
$1.00 for More-Than-a-Pound box. We'll pay expressage.
H. O. WILBUR & SONS, Inc., Philadelphia, Pa.

Four panel advertising sheet for "Wilbur's Chocolate and Cocoa Products of Excellence" (including the famous Wilbur Buds that were already "too well known to need an introduction"), paper mounted on foam board. 10" x 5.5". $10-20.

This 1911 ad for Wilbur's Chocolate Buds appeared in *Cosmopolitan* magazine. Magazine advertising was an important means of obtaining national recognition for companies and their products. $10-15.

Black and white photograph of Wilbur auto carrying "Candy Day" message from Philadelphia to San Francisco. Note Independence Square in background and date of October 14 on car. Photograph, $75-100.

Independence Square—Showing Wilbur Auto Carrying
Candy Day Message from Phila. to San Francisco

"Display is a style factor which changes day to day. Years ago, someone discovered that colored satins made a good background for candy. Most confectioners invested heavily in that material, and some use satin exclusively to this day. In the meantime, many new and attractive materials have come into the picture . . .

One favorite material is a combination of crepe paper and colored cellophane. For quickly changing seasonal displays this combination is ideal for counter and case displays. White crepe paper covered with red cellophane makes a rich and clean background for Valentine displays. Red, white and blue crepe paper, covered with colorless cellophane is good for Washington's Birthday and other patriotic occasions. Yellow crepe with yellow cellophane makes a nice background for Easter Eggs . . .

Display is one method of merchandising which pays immediate dividends in direct proportion to the attention it receives, since experts estimate that 85% of all candy is bought on impulse. There is no excuse for anyone in a candy shop being idle at any time, for when today's displays—window and store—have been completed, there is always tomorrow's display to be designed and built." (*Confectioners' 1939 Year Book*, Retail Confectioners' Association of Philadelphia, Inc.)

Black and white photograph of 1919 Wilbur Chocolate window display, with the stirring cupid logo prominently featured in the center. Photograph, $50-75.

Framed advertisement for Ideal Cocoa, sepia tone woman holding cocoa tin and chocolate bar. 10" x 13.5". $50-75.

Small ad with gold lettering for the Ideal Chocolate Company, "The name IDEAL guarantees the highest quality and absolute purity." $10-15.

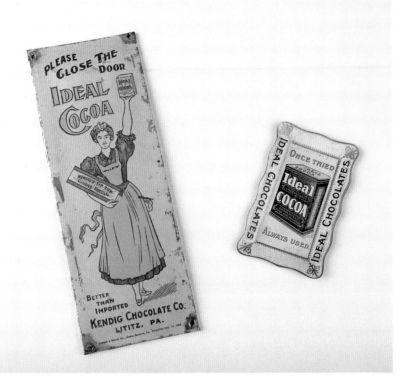

Small metal door plate advertising Ideal Cocoa, "Better than imported," Kendig Chocolate Co., Lititz, Pa., 8.25" long, $150-200; small tin tray, also advertising Ideal Cocoa, "Once Tried, Always Used," $100-150.

Below:
Advertising card for the Noah's Arks, noting that "the combination of toy and delicious chocolate in animal forms is something no child can resist." $20-25.

Framed dealer advertisement for Ideal Noah's Arks, with illustration of a chocolate animal and the ark shaped package, c. 1922. These novelties were among the most popular made by the Ideal Cocoa and Chocolate Co.; the colorful, animal theme box can be seen on page 51. 9" x 11.5". $35-50.

Large cardboard sign advertising "Suchard famous Bittra semi-sweet chocolate" with illustration of coin-operated vending machine. 21" x 11". $50-75.

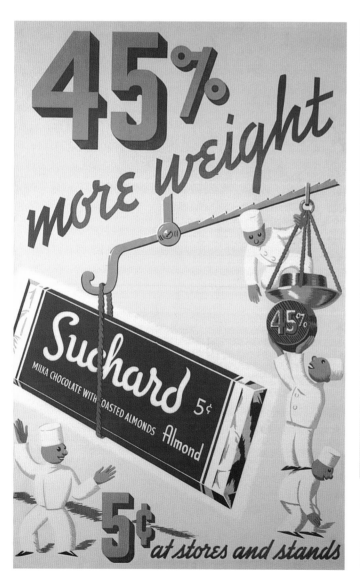

Copy of an advertising cut for Suchard candy bars, announcing
"Bigger Bars" and "New Wrappers." 7.75" x 9.9". $10-20.

Large sign advertising Suchard Milka Chocolate with
Roasted Almonds, c. 1932. 29.5" x 45". $125-175.

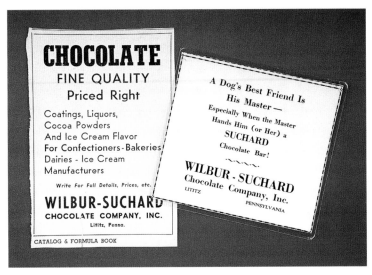

Two paper advertisements from the Wilbur-Suchard
Chocolate Company, Inc., Lititz, Pa., one tailored for the
wholesale market and one for the retail market. $10 ea.

Once in a while one finds
a picture which tells a story
far better than words—

and we think we have
found one which perfectly
portrays the chocolate
business in 1943!–

Below and right:
1943 advertising sheet with black and white photograph of two
children and Suchard chocolate wrapper. 17" x 11" (folded). $15-20.

These two black and white photographs show Wilbur-Suchard's advertising for Suchard Milk Chocolate With Almonds on the side of a delivery truck and the side of a painted plank wooden fence. Photographs, $20-25 ea.

Black and white photograph of a young girl with pigtails eating a Suchard candy bar. As the next three photos illustrate, she was meant to represent "Sue Shard," an advertising character for the Wilbur-Suchard Chocolate Company. 8" x 10.25". $20-30.

A drawing of "Sue Shard," the little pigtailed girl, appears on this box for Suchard chocolate bars. An undated promotional piece for Wilbur-Suchard notes that "recently the Company adopted a small child advertising character known as 'Sue Shard.' 'Sue' with her pigtails and little cap, shown eating with some gusto a Suchard Milk Chocolate bar, has become a national character. Incidentally, according to Company spokesman, she has helped educate people in the proper pronounciation [sic] of the name of its product." 4.6" x 7.4". $15-20.

Enameled tin sign advertising Suchard chocolate, with illustration of "Sue Shard" at upper right and four corner holes for nails. 5.2" x 7". $50-75.

A Santa version of "Sue Shard" appears in this holiday greeting from Wilbur-Suchard representatives. $20-25.

Black and white advertisement, "Switzerland never had it so good," with illustration of Wilbur Buds and candy bars. Wilbur Chocolate Co., Inc., Lititz, Pennsylvania. $15-20.

Small, tip size tray depicting the inside of Wilbur Chocolate's Candy Americana Museum, Lititz, Penna. 7" x 4.5". $10-15.

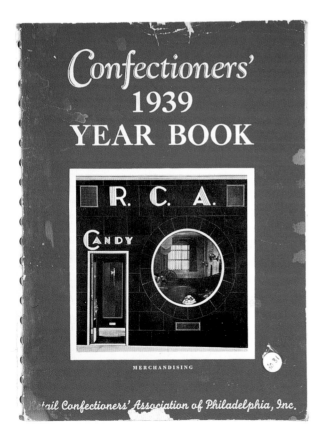

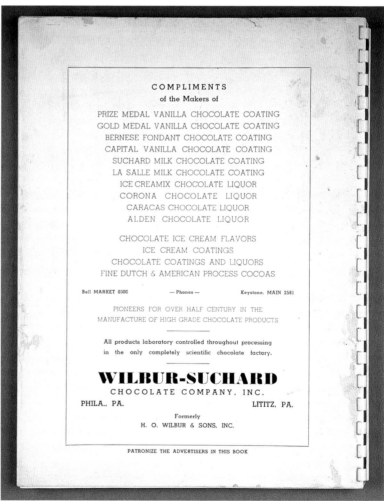

Left and above:
Wilbur-Suchard obtained prime advertising space for its chocolate coatings and other products on the back cover of this *Confectioners' 1939 Year Book* published by the Retail Confectioners' Association of Philadelphia, Inc. $25-30.

Below and right:
Two large advertising signs from the Wilbur Chocolate Company, c. 1980s. One provides statistical information about Wilbur's primary business, the other lists important dates in Wilbur's history from 1884 to 1986. 46" high ea.

"kay Besser Chorlat, kay Blotz in de Welt, -as doe."

1884-Company founded as H.O. Wilbur & Sons, Phila.

1893-WILBUR BUDS First Made and Sold.

1928-Name changed to Wilbur-Suchard Chocolate Co.

1930-Company moved to Lititz from Philadelphia.

1951-Wilbur pioneered first shipment of liquid chocolate.

1958-Name changed to Wilbur Chocolate Co., Inc.

1968-Wilbur Chocolate Co., Inc. became a subsidiary of MacAndrews & Forbes Co., Philadelphia.

1986-Wilbur became a subsidiary of Ambrit, Inc.

"No Better Chocolate, nowhere in the world -as here."

Wilbur® CHOCOLATE

Did you know...

Wilbur Chocolate's primary business is manufacturing. Currently, Wilbur produces over 120 million pounds of chocolate and confectionery ingredients each year for the nations bakers confectioners and dairies.

Approximately 70 million pounds of cocoa beans, 40 million pounds of sugar, and six million pounds of milk products are used each year to create the smooth, rich flavor of Wilbur Chocolate.

This advertisement for Wilbur's chocolate coatings appeared in the October, 1989 issue of *Candy Industry*. The same issue featured an article titled "Wilbur's breaks ground with dual roast system," noting that "Wilbur Chocolate Co. has built perhaps the most state-of-the-art chocolate liquor production operation in the United States with its new $10-million facility in Mount Joy, PA."

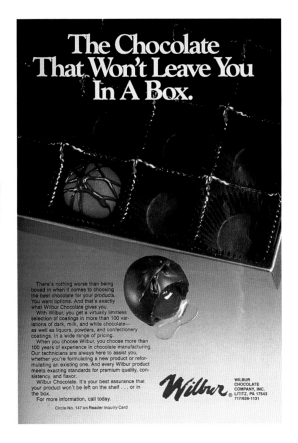

Below and right:
Color catalog of Wilbur Chocolate products, 8 pages and covers. 5.5" x 8.5". $10-20.

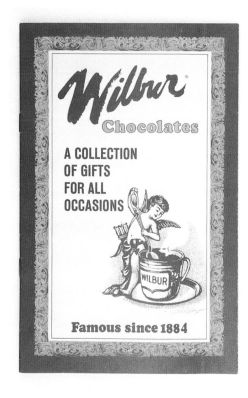

Newspaper advertisement from 1972 announcing the opening of "Wilbur Chocolate's Factory Outlet Store" in Lititz, Pa. 1.75" x 4". $10.

Three color lithographed tradecards for Croft, Wilbur & Co., 1226 Market Street, Philadelphia, with appealing images of children. 2.75" x 4.25", $10-12 ea.

Two small tradecards or insert cards, both decorated with flowers and reading "Compliments of Croft, Wilbur & Co." $10-12 ea.

Color lithographed tradecard for Croft, Wilbur & Co. with two children riding a candy see-saw. 2.75" x 4.25". $25-35.

Right and below:
These six advertising postcards from H.O. Wilbur & Sons all advertise Wilbur's Milk Chocolate and depict the cupid used in the company's logo pursuing various activities. The cards are marked with different Series numbers; note the patriotic reference on one to "the first *real* American milk chocolate." 3.5" x 5.5" ea. Auto card: $25. All others: $10-20 ea.

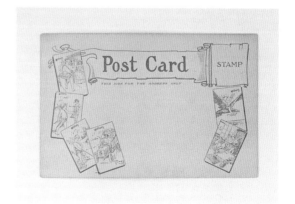

Reverse of the Wilbur advertising postcards.

These two framed tradecards feature the stirring cupid in more familiar poses, accompanied by a handwritten poem entitled "Ten Little Cupids." $15-20 ea.

Two children compete for a cup of Wilbur's Cocoa in this tradecard from H.O. Wilbur & Sons. $10-15.

This die-cut tradecard features the same two children shown from the back. $15-20.

Advertising postcard from H.O. Wilbur & Sons, showing enthusiastic visitors to the company's chocolate and cocoa refreshment booth. Note the stirring cupid perched high atop the booth. $10-12.

Advertising tradecard for "Wilbur's Chocolate Buds, H. O. Wilbur & Sons, Philadelphia U.S.A," with black and white photograph of three girls in European dress. 4" x 4". $15-20.

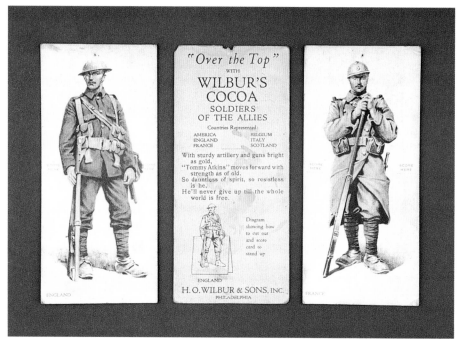

Left and below:
Wilbur's Cocoa "Soldier of the Allies" cards, depicting World War I soldiers in uniforms of England, France, Scotland, Italy, and America, H.O. Wilbur & Sons, Philadelphia, Pa. A card with a soldier from Belgium was also part of this color lithographed series. 2.5" x 5.25", $15-20 ea.

Advertising card for assorted Wilbur Buds. Back reads: "Vanilla Dark Sweet, Continental Milk, Semisweet Mint, Favorites for all occasions. Unusual gifts, exceptional desserts, delightful snacks—CHOCOLATE at its best. Made by Pennsylvania Dutch craftsmen for over 85 years. Wilbur Chocolate Co., Inc. Subsidiary MacAndrews & Forbes Co., Lititz, Pa. 17543." $5-7.

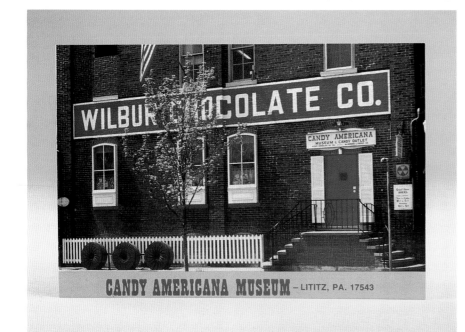

Left and below:
Two contemporary postcards showing the Wilbur Chocolate Co. Candy Americana Museum and Candy Outlet. Back of each reads: "Free admission to the museum showing the history and romance of the candy industry since revolutionary times."

Recipe Booklets

Recipe booklets were commonly used as an advertising strategy by food companies of the late nineteenth century. They provided information to homemakers while encouraging the sale of products used in the recipes.

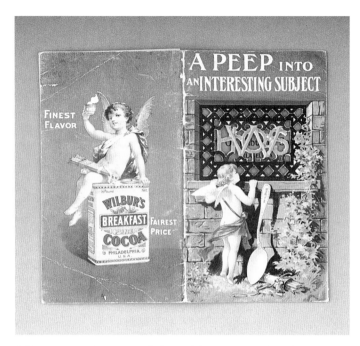

A Peep into an Interesting Subject, 26 page recipe booklet written by Agnes H. Reigart and Mabel R. Dulon, copyright 1904 by H. O. Wilbur & Sons. 3.4" x 5.75". $15-20.

Inside pages from *A Peep into an Interesting Subject*.

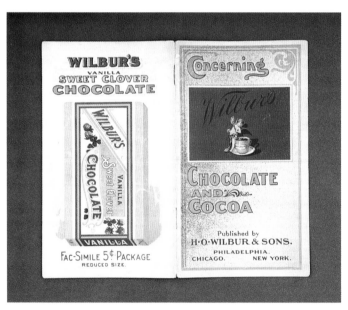

Concerning Wilbur's Chocolate and Cocoa, 22 page advertising and recipe booklet containing "Recipes for Wilbur's Cocoa and Chocolate by Agnes H. Reigart and Mabel R. Dulon," copyright 1904 by H.O. Wilbur & Sons. 3.3" x 5.75". $10-15.

Cooks' Tours through Wilburland, 40 page recipe booklet, c. 1912. 3.25" x 6.25". $15-25.

Two die-cut recipe booklets, one for Wilbur's Cocoa *Conservation Recipes,* 8 pages, c. 1912, $40-60; the other for Wilbur's Cocoa *War-Time Recipes,* 12 pages, c. 1920s, $15-20. The inside front cover of the *War-Time Recipes* booklet contains encouragement for cooks to "[h]elp the Government in the conservation of meat, flour and other articles of food required to win the war by trying one or more of the following recipes, and find what palatable and nutritive foods can be made with cocoa. 3.25" x 4.5" ea.

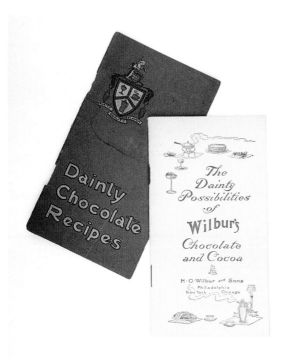

Dainty Chocolate Recipes, advertising and recipe booklet from H.O. Wilbur & Sons, brown paper with silver and black printing. 3.4" x 6.25". $10-15.

Two inside pages from *Dainty Chocolate Recipes,* appealing to the universal desire for a good night's sleep as incentive to drink a "soothing cup" of cocoa.

Tall, cylinder style glass vending machine made by the National Vending Machine Co. for H.O. Wilbur & Son, patented 1904. "Wilbur's Double Extra Vanilla Chocolate, 1¢." This same style vending machine was also used for Chiclets Gum and Colgan's Taffy Tolu. 15" h. $300-450.

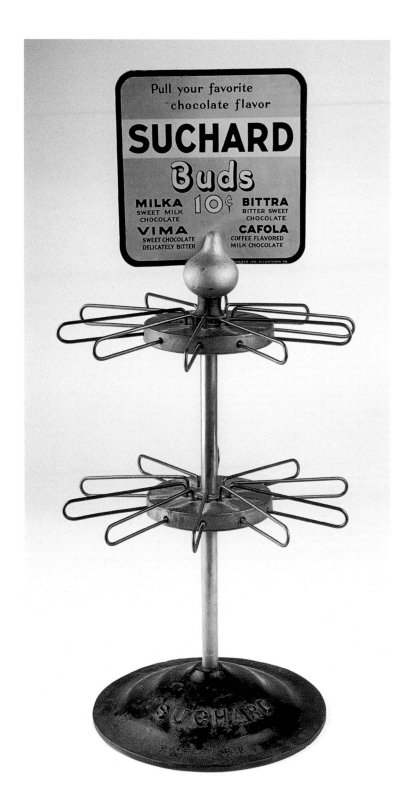

Metal display stand for four different kinds of Suchard Buds, "Pull your favorite chocolate flavor." 19" high, 8.25" dia. base. $100-150.

Wall mounted vending machine for Wilburmilk, 5¢ milk chocolate candy bars. 4.5" x 32". $250-350.

Premiums and Promotions

Chocolate companies, like many others, recognized the value of offering special promotions with their products early on. Free samples, prizes, and useful objects featuring the company's name or logo were (and are) effective ways to keep a product fresh in customers' minds and build brand name loyalty.

Two tin broom holders advertising Wilbur's Cocoa, H. O. Wilbur & Sons, Inc., Philadelphia, Pa. 2.5" x 3.75" plus wire ring holder. Left: $150-250. Right: $50-75.

Wilbur's Drawing Book, compliments of H.O. Wilbur & Sons, included instructions for receiving "a cake of Wilbur's American Milk Chocolate Free." 3.5" x 5.75". $25-35.

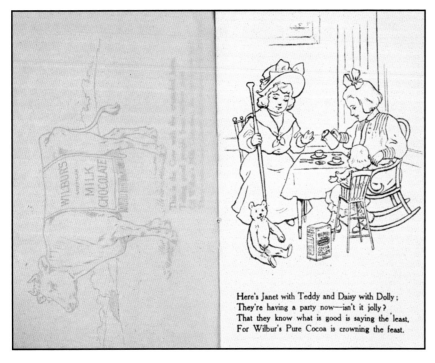

The inside of *Wilbur's Drawing Book* has ten pages of drawings and poems divided by ten pages of tracing paper.

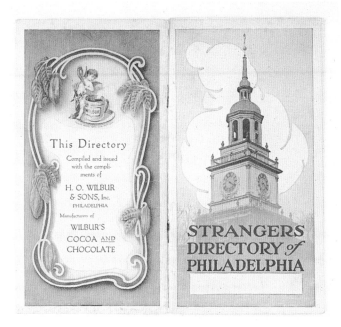

This advertising card from H.O. Wilbur & Sons features Little "Will-Burr," a "Strong, Healthy Little Man who drinks lots of Wilbur's Cocoa." The reverse of the card includes instructions for receiving six suits of clothes in exchange for Wilbur labels. 2.5" x 5.3". $15-20.

Strangers Directory of Philadelphia, a 24 page booklet "compiled and issued with the compliments of H. O. Wilbur & Sons, Inc." includes pull-out Rand McNally maps of Philadelphia and Atlantic City plus facts and points of interest for visitors. 3.4" x 6.4". $5-15.

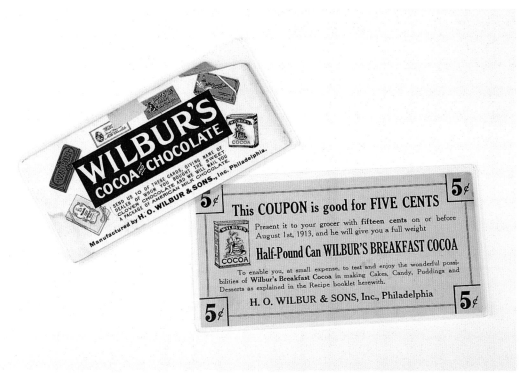

Left: Promotional card from H.O. Wilbur & Sons, Inc., inviting the consumer to "Send us 10 of these cards, giving name of dealer of whom you bought the sweet clover chocolate and we will mail you a package of American milk chocolate." Right: Coupon for five cents off a "Half-Pound Can Wilbur's Breakfast Cocoa," distributed by H.O. Wilbur & Sons, Inc., Philadelphia. Note expiration date of August 1, 1913. $10-12 ea.

Three baseball cards advertising the Kendig Chocolate Co., Lititz, Pa., with photographs of players Frank Gilhooley, Lee Magee, and George Cutshaw. 2" x 3", $30 each.

Above and right:
Promotion slip and label for 1 oz. bar of Mickey Mouse Toasted Nut Chocolate, featuring offer for "A Mickey Mouse Boy's Watch Or Girl's Mesh Bag Free" from the Wilbur-Suchard Chocolate Co., c. 1930s. Other gifts were also available, as listed on the promotion slip. 4.5" x 4.5". $75-125.

PLUTO – THE PUP

A $1.50 Boy's Mickey Mouse Pocket Watch or a Girl's Stunning Mesh Bag will be delivered free to every boy or girl who sends us five (5) wrappers showing a picture of a different character on the *inside* of each label.

Or you may send us four (4) wrappers showing a picture of a different character on the *inside* of each wrapper, and we will send you *free* your choice of any one of the following attractive gifts—

Large Cut-Out Doll Book
Large Coloring Book
Package of Stationery
62-Page Movie Story Book
The Big Little Book
7-Piece Metal Tea Set
Mickey Mouse Art Set

If you care to, you may send us four (4) different labels and 50c. for the Watch or Mesh Bag or three (3) different labels and 10c. for your choice of the other gifts.

WILBUR-SUCHARD CHOCOLATE CO.
PHILA., PA.

3LJ

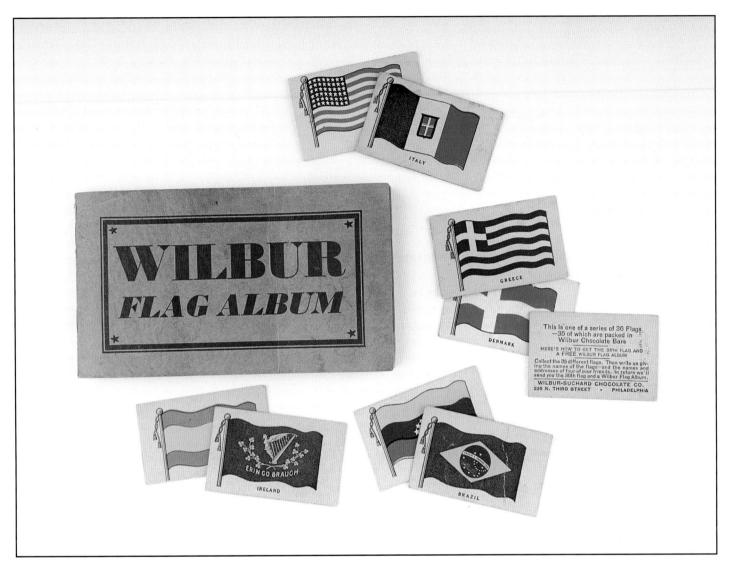

Wilbur Flag Album and individual flag cards, each containing instructions on the reverse side for obtaining the last flag in the series plus a free album. The cards were packed inside chocolate bars made by the Wilbur-Suchard Chocolate Co. Album 5.9" x 3.25". $20-35.

A trio of metal thimbles advertising Wilbur's Cocoa. $10-15 ea.

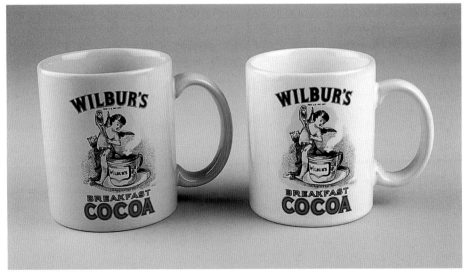

Pair of ceramic mugs advertising Wilbur's Breakfast Cocoa, one in cream and one in white. These and the other ceramic and glass items that follow have all been sold recently in Wilbur's candy store. Although some can be found on current Internet auction sites, they are too new in general to have an established secondary market value. 3.5" high.

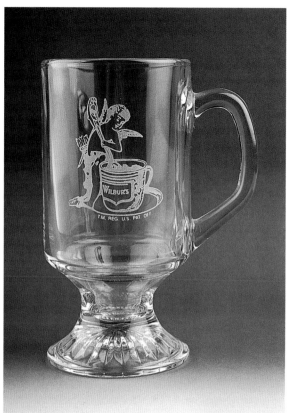

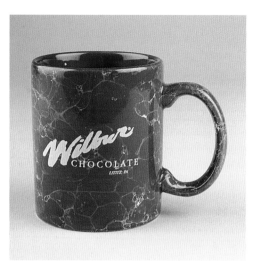

Contemporary ceramic mug, "Wilbur Chocolate, Lititz, Pa.," c. 1990s. 3.5" high.

Above and right:
Contemporary glass mug and tumbler, each decorated with Wilbur's stirring cupid logo on front. Mug: 5.5" high. Tumbler: 3.5" high.

Contemporary ceramic latte mug, with simple brown printing on cream background. 3.5" high x 4.5 dia.

Contemporary ceramic plate advertising Wilbur's Breakfast Cocoa, 8.5" dia. "Made exclusively for Wilbur's Chocolate Co." is printed on the back.

Contemporary ceramic crock, "Wilbur's / Since 1884." 7" high.

A smaller ceramic crock, also contemporary, with Wilbur logo on the front. 3.75" high.

Pair of Wilbur's Chocolate Nostalgia Jigsaw Puzzles, 18" x 24" finished size each.

Child's coloring book from Wilbur's Candy Americana Museum, shown with recipe booklet entitled *Wilbur Chocolate Flavorful Treasures, Past and Present*. Coloring book: 8" x 10.75". Recipe booklet: 5" x 7.5".

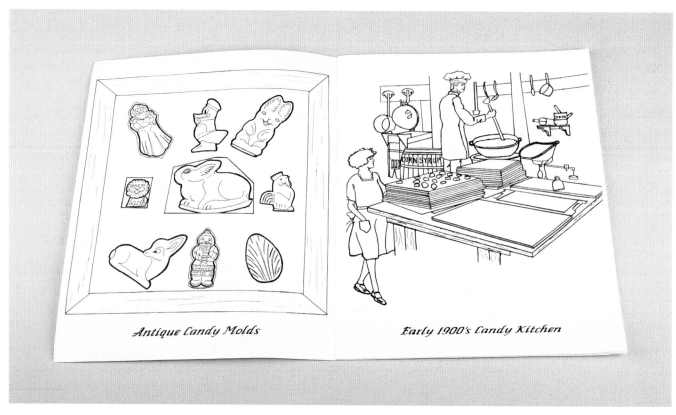

Two inside pages from the Wilbur coloring book.

Address book with accordion pages advertising the Wilbur Chocolate Co., shown with notecard illustrating the contemporary Wilbur factory.

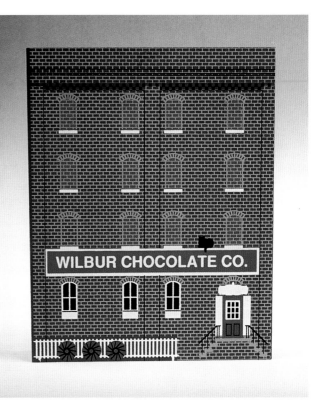

Wooden replica of Wilbur Chocolate's red brick building, made by The Cat's Meow, © 1993. 5" x 4".

Two sets of promotional card decks advertising Wilbur Chocolate.

Two pair of promotional refrigerator magnets for Wilbur Chocolate, one with color illustrations of the cupid logo, the other with stylized drawings of a Wilbur Bud.

111

Miniature Wilbur refrigerator truck made by Winross, illustrated with the stirring cupid logo and two Wilbur Buds, c. 1991. 10" x 2.25". $40-60.

Miniature Wilbur tanker truck, also made by Winross. 9.5" x 1.75". $35-45.

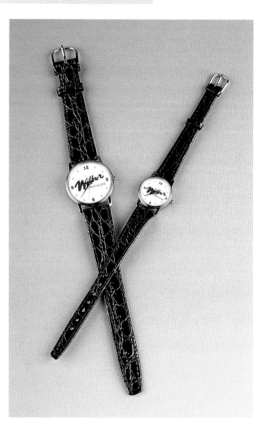

Promotional watches for men and women, with contemporary style "Wilbur" lettering across face.

Two pair of metal lapel pins advertising the Wilbur Chocolate Company.

Adhesive bandage carrier and level with tape measure, both promotional items advertising the Wilbur Chocolate Co.

Promotional spoon with Wilbur stirring cupid logo at one end. 5" long.

Metal ornaments from 1995 and 1996, each with Wilbur Chocolate stirring cupid logo. Round ornament: 3" dia. Bell ornament: 3.5" x 3".

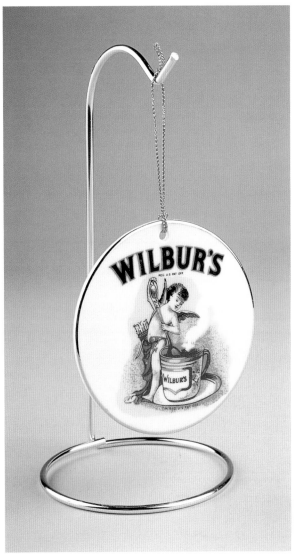

Decorative ornament on stand, also with stirring cupid logo. 3" dia.

Left:
Mini shopping bag made of burlap sold at Wilbur's Candy Americana Museum. 5.75" high.

Pinback button for fans of Wilbur Chocolate! 2.5" dia.

Chapter Five
Chocolate Pots

As we have seen, chocolate for many years was a drink of the elite; it was not until relatively late in its history that chocolate became widespread enough to be enjoyed by those of all social levels. In the fashionable homes of the upper echelon, elegant porcelain chocolate pots were used for serving this equally elegant beverage. Although found in various shapes and sizes, chocolate pots are generally tall and slender with a short spout at the top that distinguishes them from their long-spouted cousins, the teapots. They often have an opening in the finial used for inserting a swizzle stick or spoon to stir the hot beverage inside. Chocolate sets may include a pot, six or eight tall chocolate cups, a creamer and sugar, and tray.

Left: White chocolate pot with small lavender roses, marked with green eagle, "CT, Germany." 9.5" high. Center: White chocolate pot with bright pink flowers, gold leaf, unmarked. 9.5" high. Right: White chocolate pot with pink roses and green fluted top and bottom, marked "No. 1000, MZ Austria, Green Eagle." 9.5" high. $75-150 ea.

White chocolate pot with dark green at top and gold leaf, unmarked. 10.5" high. $50-100.

Left: Pink and white chocolate pot with pink roses, marked "Germany 178, WZ : 34." 10" high. Right: Green and white chocolate pot with rose colored flowers, unmarked. 10" high. $75-150 ea.

Left: White chocolate pot with yellow and pink roses, unmarked. 10" high. Right: White chocolate pot with turquoise blue lid, handle, and spout, unmarked. 10" high. $50-75 ea.

From left: White chocolate pot with pink flowers and gold leaf, marked "A Lanternier, Limoges France." 9" high; white chocolate pot with yellow and pink flowers, pale pink at handle. 8" high; white chocolate pot with pink carnations, scalloped edge and base, marked "Brunswick Germany." 10" high; white chocolate pot with swirl design and pink roses. 9.5" high. $175-200 ea.

Left: Pale pink and white chocolate pot with fancy handle and top, unmarked. 9" high. Right: White chocolate pot with pink and blue carnations, marked "A Lantemier & Co., Limoges A/L France." 10" high. $175-200 ea.

White chocolate pot with pink hydrangeas, scalloped top, base and handle, marked "Brunswick, Germany." 10" high. $100-150.

Pink and white chocolate pot with pale flowers and fluted
base, marked "M & C L France." 9.5" high. $100-150.

Chocolate pot with pale flowers and gold leaf decoration,
marked "Haviland, France, Limoges." 10.5 " high. $100-150.

White chocolate pot with yellow daisies and scalloped base,
marked "Bavarian china, Germany." 9.5" high. $75-100.

White chocolate pot set with matching cup and saucer, small pink
flowers in trellis design, marked "Limoges." Pot: 9" high. $125-175.

Opposite page top:
A trio of chocolate pots with bold flower designs. Left: White with very large yellow rose, marked "Alice, JR Wavenia." 9" high. Center: Pale green with large dogwood blossom and gold leaf handle, marked "Royal Murich handpainted." 10.5" high. Right: Two large sunflowers and brown trim, marked "hand painted Nippon." 10" high. $200-225 ea.

Opposite page bottom:
Tall yellow chocolate pot with pink flowers, three matching cups and saucers, marked "Germany." $100-150.

Left: Yellow and white chocolate pot with large pink roses, marked "Kamla, Germany." 10" high. Right: Pale yellow chocolate pot with square spout, white flowers, gold edging, marked "A H Wasser, Silesia." 9.5" high. $125-150 ea.

White chocolate pot with green leaves on tea pot shape, marked "CFH / QDM, France" and "CH Field / Haviland / Limoges." 9" high. $125-150.

White chocolate pot with pale flowers, marked "Sevres Germany." 9" high. $150-200.

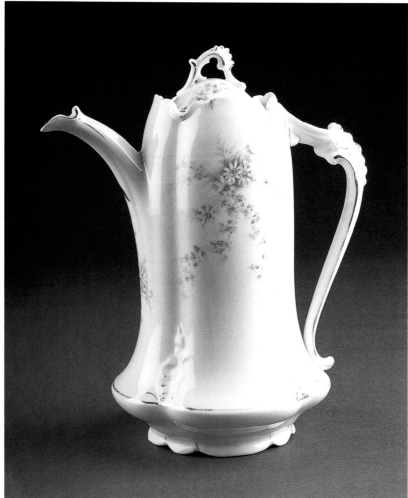

White chocolate pot with pale green top and bottom, small green and rose flowers, marked "2440." 10" high. $75-100.

Left: White chocolate pot with large pink rose and gold base. Right: White chocolate pot with dark pink roses, marked "175." $125-150.

Left: White chocolate pot with long spout and fancy roses, unmarked. 9.5" high. Right: White chocolate pot with roses and gold scalloped edging at top. 10" high. $75-100 ea.

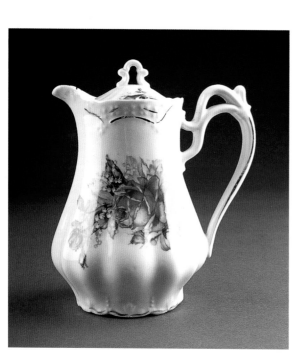

White chocolate pot with large red rose decoration, unmarked. $75-100.

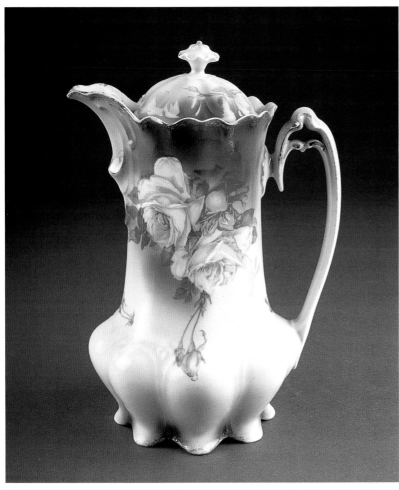

White, rose, and green chocolate pot with flowers and scalloped base, marked "Carlsbad Austria, 933 M.Z." 10" high. $100-150.

Below:
Left: White chocolate pot with large pink and yellow roses, gold handle and top, marked "6144 - 45". 9" high. Center: White and rose chocolate pot with pink pansies and lustre, marked "Limoges / Porcelain." 10" high. Right: Pink, green, orange, and white chocolate pot with large roses, gold lustre handle and top, unmarked. 9" high. $175-200 ea.

Pale yellow chocolate pot with rose colored base, yellow and pink roses, marked "Hand painted, Made in Germany." 9" high. $75-125.

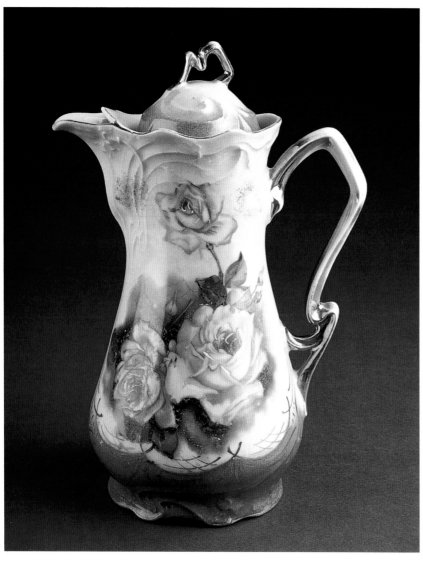

Yellow and rose chocolate pot with large pink and yellow roses, rose lustre handle and spout, marked "Handpainted, Made in Germany." 10" high. $75-125.

White chocolate pot with multicolored flowers and royal blue at top, base, and handle, unmarked. 10" high. $50-75.

Very ornate chocolate pot with bright blue top and bottom, gold trim, and two large roses, marked "HAND, SNB, Painted." 10" high. $75-100.

Maroon and white chocolate pot with rose and lavender flowers, unmarked. 8" high. $50-75.

Cream and white chocolate pot with large pink flowers. 9.5" high. $50-75.

Left: White chocolate pot with green leaves, marked "RS Prussia." 10" high. Right: White chocolate pot with pink top, yellow and pink flowers, marked "Austria." 10.5" high. $300-400 ea.

Left: White chocolate pot with small roses, gold leaf on spout and handle, marked "Elite, Limoges France." 9.5" high. Center: White chocolate pot with only a few flowers and gold leaf handle, marked "Limoges W lpouwat France." 11" high. Right: White chocolate pot with flowers and fluted base, marked "Haviland France, Haviland Limoges." 8.5" high. $200-250 ea.

Left: Orange and green chocolate pot with large red rose in center, unmarked. 10" high. Center: White chocolate pot with orange spout and top, pink and yellow flowers, unmarked. 9.5" high. Right: White chocolate pot with tan around top and purple roses, marked "660." 10" high. $150-175 ea.

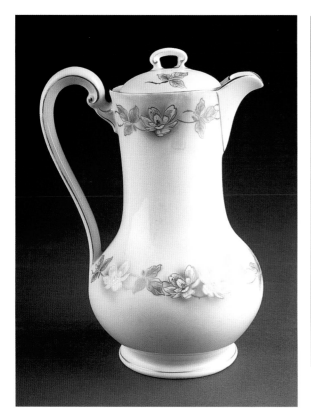

White chocolate pot with small gold and white flowers, marked "Weimar, Germany." 10" high. $100-150.

Left: White chocolate pot with large pink roses and gold edging, marked "Made in Germany, 1465." 10" high. Right: White chocolate pot with green spout and pink carnations, unmarked. 10" high. $100-150 ea.

White chocolate pot with purple flowers and gold trim, marked "Victoria." 10" high. $50-100.

Left: White chocolate pot with violets and long spout, marked "5008." 9" high. Center: White chocolate pot with violets, unmarked. 10" high. Right: White chocolate pot with pink and purple flowers, marked "Welmar Germany." 9.5" high. $100-150 ea.

Chocolate pot with pale flowers and gold leaf decoration, marked "Haviland France, Limoges." 11" high. $75-100.

Green and white chocolate pot with gold leaf, marked "Porcelain, Thomas Haviland Limoges, France." 10.5" high. $75-100.

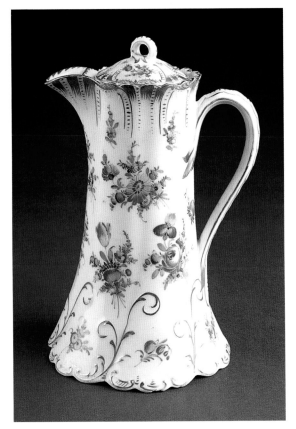

Chocolate pot painted in shades of yellow, green, and rose, gold leaf top and handle, marked "Warwick China." 11" high. $75-100.

White chocolate pot with multicolor flowers and gold leaf, marked with blue mask, crown H, "Dresden." 9" high. $125-175.

White chocolate pot with pale green base, gold leaf on flowers, top and handle, marked "Limoges France." 10" high. $100-150.

White chocolate pot with pale yellow top and bottom, multicolor flowers, marked "Brunswick, Germany." 10" high. $75-100.

Left: White chocolate pot with tiny rosebuds, gold handle and top, marked "Limoges GDA, Haviland France GDA." 10" high. Right: White chocolate pot with sleek lines and flowers at top, unmarked. 9" high. $100-150 ea.

White chocolate pot with pale flowers, marked with eagle "CT Germany." 9" high. $75-100.

White chocolate pot with roses, marked "Made in Germany." 9" high. $75-100.

From left: White chocolate pot with pale green top, unmarked. 10" high; white chocolate pot with large dogwood and lustre, marked "Hand painted NIPPON." 9" high; white chocolate pot with multicolor flowers, marked "Porcelain, Germany." 10" high; white chocolate pot with small flowers, unmarked. 10" high. $150-200 ea.

White chocolate pot with large pink rose, small pink rosebuds, gold leaf handle and trim, marked "Royal Bayruth Priv 1794 Bavaria." 9.5" high. $200-250.

White chocolate pot with pink and yellow flowers around top, marked "OSEG (Royal) Austria." 9.5" high. $100-150.

Green and white chocolate pot with three matching cups and saucers, marked "Noritake." 11" high (pot). $75-100.

Chocolate pot with painted flowers and gold leaf, marked "D & C France." 9.5 "high. $75-100.

Left: White chocolate pot with oriental motif, blue at top, base, and handle, unmarked. 9.5" high.
Right: White chocolate pot with royal blue top and base, pink and purple flowers, marked "Hand painted Nippon." 9" high. $150-200 ea.

White chocolate pot with oriental motif, blue handle and trim, unmarked. 8.5" high. $50-100.

Two chocolate pots with oriental motifs. Left: White pot with rust top, base, and handle. 8.5" high. Right: Cream pot with gold and rust, oriental mark. 10" high. $150-175 ea.

Oriental motif chocolate pot with figures and flowers outlined in black, unmarked. 9.5" high. $50-75.

Detail of outlined figures and flowers.

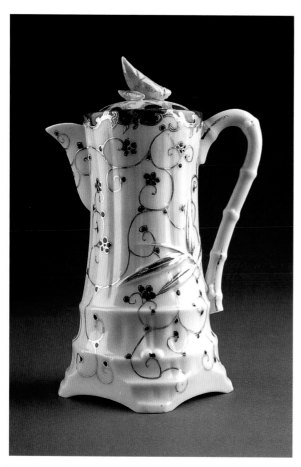

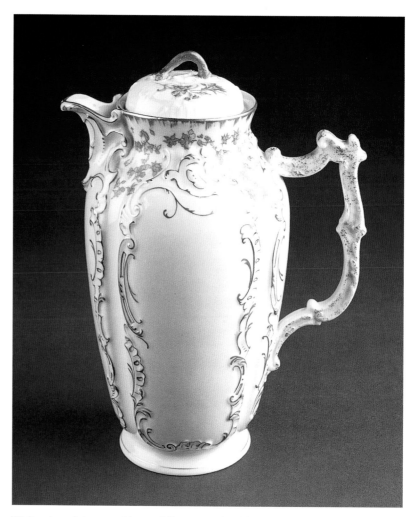

White chocolate pot with blue and gold decoration, two turquoise and yellow parakeets on top. 9" high. $100-150.

White chocolate pot with small flowers and gold leaf decoration, marked "LS & S Carlsbad Austria." 11" high. $75-100.

Left: Ivory chocolate pot in square shape with daisies, gold leaf edging at top, and geometric motif handle, marked "3547 / 19." 10" high. Right: White chocolate pot with gold flecks and stylized bird design. 10" high. $100-150 ea.

Detail of bird design.

White ridged chocolate pot with roses around very top, marked "Wurteenbeer 19." $100-150.

Ivory chocolate pot with small single roses, faded gold lustre, marked "Stoke-on-Trent (crown) England Roses." 9" high. $75-100.

Left: White chocolate pot with pink roses, marked "(green eagle) C.T." 10" high. Center: White chocolate pot with pale pink and yellow roses, marked "C. T. Germany." 10" high. Right: White chocolate pot with large pink roses, marked "Bron B Wick, Germany." 10" high. $200-250 ea.

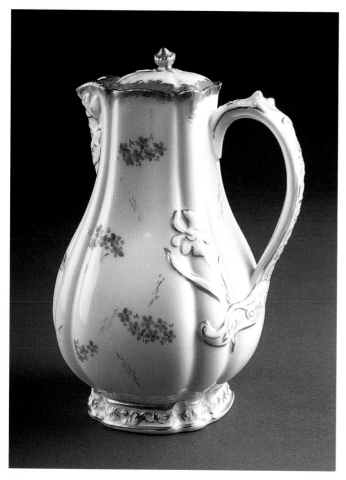

White chocolate pot with small blue flowers, gold leaf, and square top, marked "H&C/L." 10" high. $75-100.

White chocolate pot with unusual design of gold and blue circles, unmarked. 10" high. $50-75.

Left: White chocolate pot with fancy gold top and small multicolor flowers, marked "Altrohla, Austria." 10" high. Center: White chocolate pot with blue and white flowers, marked "7 / 8." 9.5" high. Right: White chocolate pot with pink and orange flowers, gold leaf rim and spout, marked "Germany (eagle) C.T." 10" high. $150-175 ea.

Left: White chocolate pot with blue pale around top and flowers above gold leaf handle, unmarked. 9" high. Right: White chocolate pot with wild flower decoration, gold handle and top, marked "GDA, France." 10" high. $100-125 ea.

White chocolate pot with banding around top and base, small flowers enclosed in ovals, marked "Nippon." 9" high. $100-125.

Left: White chocolate pot with blue and green at top, unmarked. 10" high. Center: Blue and yellow chocolate pot with large pink roses, marked "Chrysanthem, Bavaria." 9.5" high. Right: Dark green chocolate pot with pink roses, unmarked. 10" high. $50-100 ea.

Left: Green and white chocolate pot with pink roses, marked "Bavaria A & A." 9" high. Center: Cream and green chocolate pot with roses in center, marked "TKC Bavaria." 10" high. Right: Green and white chocolate pot with pink roses, marked "PROV SE ES Germany." 10" high. $100-125 ea.

White and rose chocolate pot with flowers, marked "Three crown China, Germany." $50-75.

Left: White chocolate pot with flowers and pale green edging, marked "Fidelia, Germany 170/49." 9" high. Center: White chocolate pot with bouquet of flowers, unmarked. 10" high. Right: White chocolate pot with small pink flowers and gold leaf, marked "Haviland Limoges France." 9" high. $125-150 ea.

Left: White chocolate pot with pink and blue flowers, pale pink at top, marked "Germany." 9" high. Center: White and green chocolate pot with white flowers, marked "Prussia." 9.5" high. Right: White chocolate pot with pale pink flowers, fluted top, and gold lines, marked "Made in Germany." 9" high. $175-250 ea.

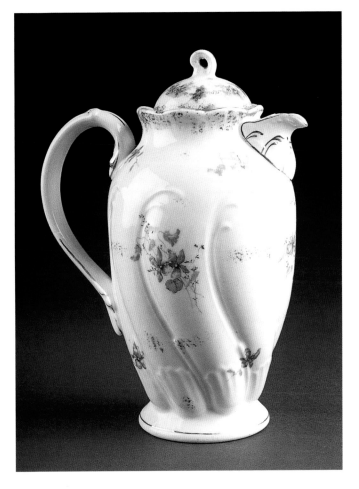

White chocolate pot with tiny violets, marked "Austria LS & S Carlsbad." 9.5" high. $100-125.

Left: White chocolate pot with orange and yellow wild roses, unmarked. 10" high. Right: White chocolate pot with orange flowers, marked "Nippon." 10" high. $75-100 ea.

Chocolate pot by Noritake, with lake scene on front. 9" high. $125-150.

Gray chocolate pot with black handle and top, bird and flower design, marked "Bavaria." 8.5" high. $50-100.

Oriental motif chocolate pot, blue bands flecked with gold, marked "219." 9.5" high. $50-75.

Bright yellow chocolate pot with purple iris and green leaves, orange mark. 10.5" high. $50-75.

Chapter Six
Miscellaneous

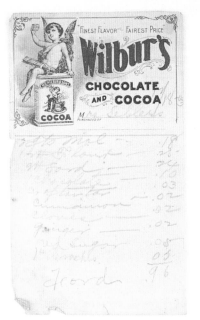

Two paper billheads with penciled shopping lists, one dated Apr 1-01, the other 12/18/03. Printed notice at the bottom of one reads: "A Supply of bill heads like this will be sent free to any grocer by writing H. O. Wilbur & Sons, Philadelphia." 4.5" x 7.5", $10-15 ea.

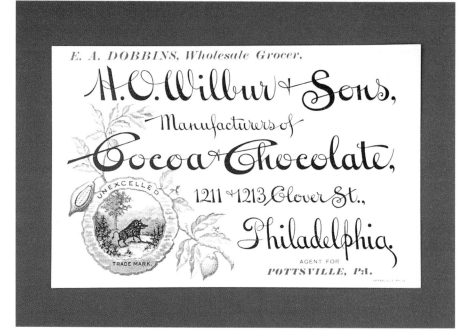

Early advertising card for "E. A. Dobbins, Wholesale Grocer, agent for Pottsville, PA.," and "H. O. Wilbur & Sons, Manufacturers of Cocoa & Chocolate." 5.5" x 3.5". $20-30.

Right and below:
Advertising brochure for *Wilbur's Cocoa & Chocolate Preparations*, color lithograph with stirring cupid sitting on crate marked "John Doe & Company, Capetown, S.A.," H.O. Wilbur & Sons. Interior marked "1909 Salesmen's Convention and Christmas Entertainment," with detailed program of minstrels, speakers, and burlesque. 3.5" x 6". $40-50.

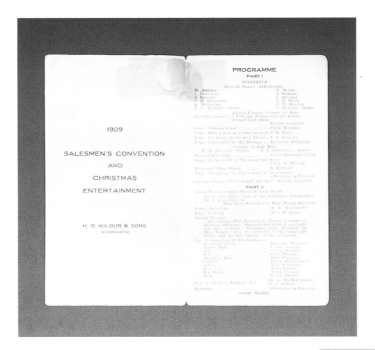

Gift enclosure and envelope from the John Wanamaker department store in Philadelphia, advising recipients that chocolate "will not keep beyond a reasonable period" and will be replaced by H.O. Wilbur & Sons, Inc. if not received in perfect condition. 3.75" x 2.7". $10-20.

149

N.° 506

H.O.WILBUR & SONS

INCORPORATED

235 NORTH THIRD STREET

PHILADELPHIA, PA.

MANUFACTURERS
COCOA AND CHOCOLATE
PRODUCTS
FACTORY
THIRD, NEW & BREAD STS.

September 14, 1925.

MEMORANDUM OF SALE

SOLD TO Mr. H. L. Young, 2809 W. Girard Ave., Phila., Pa.

2 cases Prize Medal Vanilla Chocolate Coating	@	27-1/2¢
3 cases Honeydew Milk Chocolate Coating	@	25-1/2¢
4 cases Silver Medal Vanilla Chocolate Coating	@	25¢
6 cases M. C. Milk Chocolate Coating	@	24-1/2¢
8 cases Caracas Chocolate Liquor	@	23-1/2¢
10 cases Perfection Vanilla Chocolate Coating	@	23¢
7 cases Millwood Chocolate Coating	@	19-1/2¢
5 cases Lyter Chocolate Liquor	@	18-1/2¢

TOTAL   45 cases

To be taken (in addition to sales memo. #110 and #285 expiring November 1,1925)

in approximate monthly shipments-November 2, 1925 to March 14, 1926.

TERMS: 30 days net or less 2 per cent. for payment within 10 days from date of invoice on case shipments. F.o.b., Philadelphia, actual freight allowed not exceeding   per 100 lbs.

CONDITIONS

The above prices are guaranteed against decline in seller's price list, each shipment to be billed at list price on date of shipment, but not higher than contract price.

To be taken as wanted during life of contract, with reasonable dates for shipment, and any part not previously ordered to be cancelled or shipped at seller's option, and without further notice on MARCH 14, 1926.

Customary manufacturers' clause, fire, strikes, etc., to apply to both buyers and sellers. All prices, deliveries and conditions subject to changes in so far as affected by Tariff and Taxes, commerce regulations and other eventualities beyond seller's control.

ACCEPTED: H. O. WILBUR & SONS, Inc.

W815—500 Sets (5)—9-25 S.E.
HA J 1 Co

September 14, 1925 sales memorandum for chocolate coatings and other products sold by H. O. Wilbur & Sons to Mr. H. L. Young. 8.5" x 11". $15-20.

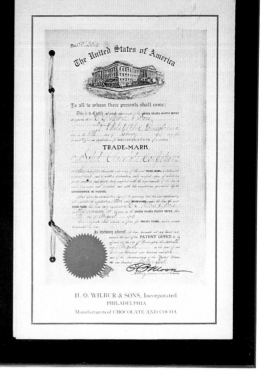

Notice to dealers regarding Wilbur's trademark for the name "Buds," shown with trademark certification issued to H.O. Wilbur & Sons, Incorporated, Philadelphia. $20-30.

Warning

TO DEALERS:

The name of **Buds**

for chocolate confections is our exclusive property and covered by trade-mark granted to us by U. S. Patent Office. A facsimile of the certificate is attached.

We hereby give WARNING that we shall protect our patrons and shall prosecute all who offer imitations for sale.

There are no Buds but WILBUR'S, and each has the name stamped on it. Insist upon getting the only genuine, WILBUR'S.

H. O. WILBUR & SONS, Inc.
PHILADELPHIA

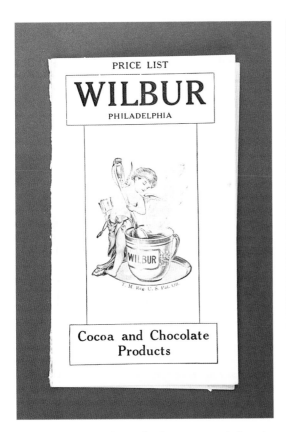

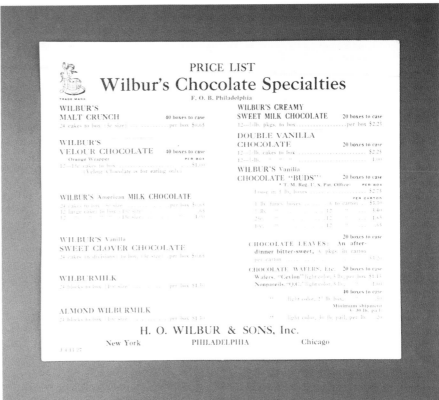

Cover and inside of price list for cocoa and chocolate products
sold by H.O. Wilbur & Sons, Inc., c. 1927 3.5" x 6". $25-35.

Box with composition samples of Wilbur milk chocolate candy
bars, part of a salesman's kit from c. 1900. H.O. Wilbur &
Sons, Inc., Philadelphia. 9.25" x 9.75". $100-150.

A trio of commemorative medallions. From left: copper colored medallion from the Philadelphia Food Exposition inscribed "Awarded to H. O. Wilbur & Sons, Premium Chocolate, 1890," 2" dia.; silver colored medallion from the Pennsylvania State Agricultural Society inscribed "Philadelphia 1884, H. O. Wilbur & Sons, Finest Cocoa and Chocolate," 2.5" dia.; and copper colored medallion from the Philadelphia Food Exposition inscribed "Awarded to H. O. Wilbur & Sons, Breakfast Chocolate & Cocoa Theta, 1890," 2" dia. $20 ea.

Left:
Pair of early glass candy jars, each labeled "Wilbur's Vanilla Chocolate Buds, H. O. Wilbur & Sons, Manufacturers, Philadelphia." 13" high ea. $100-125 ea.

Reverse of one of the glass candy jars.

Pair of tin candy compotes, right one filled with real Wilbur Buds. 8" dia. x 7" h. $75-100 ea.

Pair of smaller tin candy compotes. 4" dia. x 2.5 h. $45-60 for pair.

Underside of the smaller compote, showing Wilbur name and stirring cupid logo.

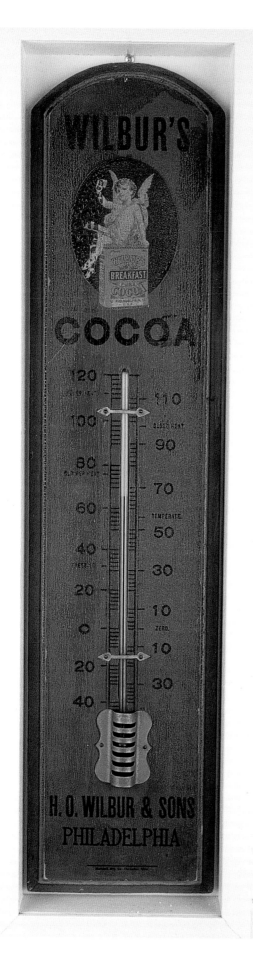

Tall wooden thermometer advertising Wilbur's Cocoa, H.O. Wilbur & Sons, Philadelphia. 5.5" x 23". $100-150.

Employee's metal check used in 1928 by H. O. Wilbur & Sons, Inc., Philadelphia. 1.4" dia. Unique item, value undetermined.

Cardboard, two-part case marked "Wilbur's Chocolate Cigarettes." 2.1" x 3". $25-35.

Ideal Chocolate And Cocoa Products booklet, published by the Ideal Cocoa & Chocolate Co. $10-15.

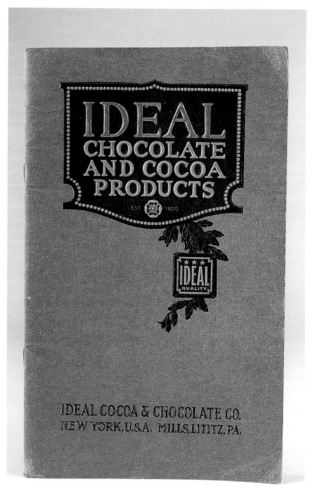

Two pinback buttons for the Wilbur-Suchard Chocolate Co., Inc. "Visitor 10," 2" dia.; "#139," 1.5" dia. $10-15 ea.

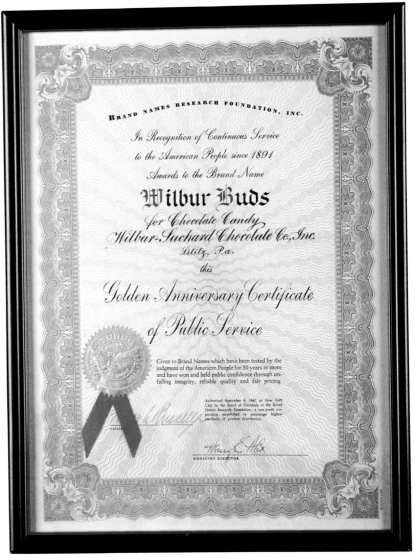

"Golden Anniversary Certificate of Public Service" awarded to the Wilbur-Suchard Chocolate Company by the Brand Names Research Foundation, Inc. in 1945. 10.5" x 13.5". $10-15.

Pair of solid chocolate "Champagne Bottles" made by the Wilbur Chocolate Company. 6" high ea.

Two issues of *Buds and Bars,* 8 page monthly newsletter of the Wilbur-Suchard Chocolate Co., Inc., one for April, 1945 and one for July, 1945. 8.4" x 11.4", $15-20 ea.

MILLIONS OF SUCHARD BARS GOING TO THE ARMED FORCES ALL OVER THE WORLD

The pictures on this and the opposite page tell a story of our Suchard bars which are going to our fighting men everywhere—in training camps, at sea, and in all the battle areas.

The upper left picture on the opposite page shows the boxes of bars being packed in special water-proof paper containers. The girls are, left to right, Wilma Stommel, Margaret Eckert, and Margaret Binder.

Upper right shows the corners of the special wooden shipping containers being painted green with a black stripe for easy identification. The girls are Mildred Nissley, Gladys Shenaberger, Rhoda Oberholtzer, Helen Donley, and Virginia Adams.

Most special packing in the center left picture with Mary Anna John, Lillian Haldeman, and Pearl Summers doing the work.

Center right shows the stencils being started on the wooden boxes, and then the outside rating. From left to right.

Kenneth Gerle, Sam Kline, Eugene Buchter, and Albert Hornberger.

Lower left Theodore Smith and John Forlow sending both empty and packed boxes upstairs on the conveyor.

Lower right, pasting on the labels

for shipment. From left to right, Wilma Stommel, Pearl Davidson, John Pekat, and Pearl Summers.

After being labelled, the boxes roll along the conveyor directly into a waiting freight car. Top picture on this page showing John Pekat, Galen Lehman, and Paul Davidson.

Middle picture on this page shows John Davidson, who boxes the entire job. And the lower picture is of a hundred box of Suchard bars ready to go overseas. Note the label.

To help the war effort as much as possible it seems that May Landes—Frank Brenner's right hand man—bought herself a pair of shoes with the new plastic soles. These soles make so much noise on pavements that May is constantly turning around to see who is following her!

Letter From a Serviceman's Mother

Dear Mrs. Bard:

Received the picture of our son Elwood yesterday and want to thank you very much for it. He looks so natural on the picture, it seems he is right here in the room with us. It will be something that I will cherish as long as I live. I only hope and pray that the day will soon come when he can be with us here to stay, and the same goes for all of the boys everywhere. So again, many thanks for the picture and I want to wish you and all the rest of the chocolate company the best of everything.

Sincerely yours,

Mrs. Sonnen.

A Wabbit Story

Once a wittle white wabbit and a wittle brown wabbit said...

Farm Life Must Have Its Charms!

...

Inside pages from the April issue of *Buds and Bars*, showing Wilbur-Suchard's production of chocolate bars for the armed forces.

All that wartime chocolate production meant employment for local residents. This newspaper advertisement from Thursday, October 26, 1944 announces job opportunities at the Wilbur-Suchard Co. in Lititz, Pennsylvania: "Help us to make more chocolate for our men and women in the armed forces." $10-15.

Solid chocolate Statue of Liberty figures made by the Wilbur Chocolate Co., c. 1986. 4" high ea.

Foil wrapped chocolate "coins," one side with stirring cupid logo, the other reading "Since 1884, Wilbur's Chocolate, Lititz, Pa. 17543." 1.5" dia. ea.

Pair of decorative Wilbur Buds made of glass, 0.75" dia. ea.

Replica of early metal compote tin containing Wilbur's Buds. 4.5" dia.

Wilbur Gourmet Chocolate Cooking Kit. Box contains recipe book, bar of Wilbur Gourmet Baking Chocolate, tin of Ideal Cocoa, and chocolate drops. 12.75" x 9".

Two styles of contemporary glass candy jars, both designed to hold Wilbur's Chocolate Buds! 5" high ea.

159

Bibliography

"A Brief History of Wilbur Chocolate Co., Inc., Lititz, Pennsylvania" (n.d., typewritten).

Bailleux, Nathalie, et. al. *The Book of Chocolate*. New York and Paris: Flammarion, 1996.

Boorstin, Daniel J. *The Americans: The Democratic Experience*. New York: Vintage Books, 1974.

Brenner, Robert. *Christmas Revisited* (Revised 2nd Edition). Atglen, PA: Schiffer Publishing, Ltd., 1999.

Broekel, Ray. *The Great American Candy Bar Book*. Boston: Houghton Mifflin Company, 1982.

——. *The Chocolate Chronicles*. Lombard, IL: Wallace-Homestead Book Company, 1985

Coe, Sophie D., and Michael D. Coe. *The True History of Chocolate*. New York: Thames and Hudson, Inc., 1996.

Congdon-Martin, Douglas. *America for Sale: A Collector's Guide to Antique Advertising*. West Chester, PA: Schiffer Publishing, Ltd., 1991.

Dezso, Douglas M., J. Leon Poirier, and Rose. D. Poirier. *Collector's Guide to Candy Containers: Identification and Values*. Paducah, KY: Collector Books, 1998.

Divone, Judene. *Chocolate Moulds: A History & Encyclopedia*. Oakton, Virginia: Oakton Hills Publications, 1987.

Fleming, Thomas. "Message in a Bottle." *Boys' Life* Vol. 88, No. 4 (April 1998): 50.

Fuller, Linda K. *Chocolate Fads, Folklore, & Fantasies: 1,000+ Chunks of Chocolate Information*. Binghamton, NY: The Harrington Park Press, 1994.

Goodrum, Charles, and Helen Dalrymple. *Advertising in America: The First 200 Years*. New York: Harry N. Abrams, Inc., 1990.

Hanes, Lorry. "It's the Wonderful World of Old Metal Chocolate Moulds." *Collectors' Eye* Vol. 1, No. 6 (November/December, 1998): 37-40.

Hershey Chocolate Corporation. *The Story of Chocolate and Cocoa*. N.p., 1926.

Jenkins, Jennifer E. "All for the Love of Chocolate." *Colonial Homes* Vol. 23, No. 5 (September 1997): 92-98.

Magee, Phyllis. "Wilbur breaks ground with dual roast system." *Candy Industry* Vol. 154, No. 10 (October, 1989): 20-26.

Magida, Phyllis. "Ghirardelli outbakes others in taste tests." *Chicago Tribune*, September 21/22, 1983.

Margolin, Victor, Ira Brichta, and Vivian Brichta. *The Promise and the Product: 200 Years of American Advertising Posters*. New York: Macmillan Publishing Co., Inc., 1979.

Muth, Henry T. "The Ideal Story" (typewritten, June 20, 1982).

Norman, Sandra J., and Karrie K. Andes. *Vintage Cookbooks and Advertising Leaflets*. Atglen, PA: Schiffer Publishing, Ltd., 1998.

Retail Confectioners' Association of Philadelphia, Inc. *Confectioners' 1939 Year Book*.

Street, Susan. N. "Tea, Coffee, Chocolate." (training manual, Conner Prairie museum, 1996).

Swift, Richard. "From Maya to Market." *New Internationalist* No. 304 (August 1998): 22-26.

"'Synonymic of excellence': Wilbur's standard for 75 yrs." *Candy Industry and Confectioner Journal*, May 12, 1959.

Teubner, Christian, et. al. *The Chocolate Bible*. New York: Penguin Putnam, Inc., 1997.

"The Story of Chocolate." http://www.candyusa.org/chocstry.html (March 13, 2000).

"The Story of the Cocoa Bean" (Wilbur-Suchard Chocolate Company, n.d., typewritten).

"Wilbur-Suchard Chocolate Company" (n.d., typewritten).

Wilbur, Ross T., compiler. "Happy Days & Special Events of the Wilbur Family: 1898-1980." N.p., 1980.

Winik, Lyric Wallwork. "Meltdown." *Forbes* Vol. 163, No. 4 (Spring 1999): 43-47.

"Why You Should Use Cocoa and Some Recipes for its Use" (n.d., typewritten).